CONTENTS

In   TING ENGLISH

Tony Wright

Edward Arnold
A member of the Hodder Headline Group
LONDON   NEW YORK   MELBOURNE   AUCKLAND

© 1994 Tony Wright

First published in Great Britain 1994

Distributed in the USA by Routledge, Chapman and Hall, Inc.
29 West 35th Street, New York, NY 10001

British Library Cataloguing in Publication Data

Wright, Tony
  Investigating English
  I. Title
  428

  ISBN 0–340–55782–6

Typeset in 11/12 point Garamond by Anneset, Weston-super-Mare
Printed and bound in Great Britain for Edward Arnold, a member of
Hodder Headline PLC, 338 Euston Road, London NW1 3BH by
Biddles Ltd., Guildford & King's Lynn.

ACKNOWLEDGEMENTS

The production of any book of learning activities designed or used either in classrooms or at home, or anywhere that a student might happen to be, involves the writer and all the colleagues and all the students with whom the activities have been developed. That is in addition to any ideas picked up from sources forgotten or of which the writer is only dimly aware. This book is no exception.

I would first like to thank colleagues who have helped me think about and develop my ideas on language awareness – Rod Bolitho, in particular, for his initial inspiration and continued support and collaboration. Also Roger Budd and Roy Taylor for their collaboration and support when the activities were in their infancy at Christ Church College, Canterbury; Sue Parker and Hazel Marshall for trialling many of them at Marjons and to Julian Edge for 'User/Analyst/Teacher', a simple but profound schema which has helped me so much to think about language awareness. I would also like to thank Peter Garrett for his comments and suggestions on an earlier draft. Any errors or inconsistencies which remain are entirely my own fault.

Many teachers in in-service workshops, language students and teacher trainees have helped me with the activities. Special mention must go to the Malaysian BEd (TESL) groups who graduated from Christ Church College, Canterbury, in 1989, 1990 and 1991; they were the original consumers of many of these activities. I hope the activities have matured and developed over the years since they first used them. More recent assistance has come at Marjons from PKG Indonesian teacher trainers, PRINSELT trainer groups, Nigerian teachers and Zambian teacher trainers. Their insights and suggestions have been of the utmost value. Finally, my thanks to the MEd (T-TELT) group of 1991–92 for their inspiration, insight and support in this venture. I only hope that the result justifies the contribution all these people have made.

Writing even a humble book of learning activities has also a personal and domestic side. Linda, Tim and Lizzie have sustained me through this task. They have also endured my absence preparing the manuscript at the computer, and the inevitable ups and downs of the writing process. Thanks are not enough.

The author and the publishers would like to thank the following for permission to use copyright material in this book:

Her Majesty's Stationery Office for weather reports from the *Guardian* Crown copyright, reproduced with the permission of the Controller of Her Majesty's

Stationery Office; the *Guardian* for extracts by Erin Sullivan, Angella Johnson, Madeleine Bunting, John Vidal and Kevin Rafferty © *Guardian*; 'English as she is mis-spoke' from *The Economist*, London, 16 July 1988; 'Common complaints – jet lag' by Tony Smith, first published in *The Independent on Sunday*, 12 July 1992; extract from *Body Time* by Gay Gaer Luce courtesy of the author; Longman Group UK for extracts from *West African Snakes* by George Cansdale, *Longman English Grammar* by L. G. Alexander, *A Communicative Grammar of English* by G. N. Leech and J. Svartvik and *A University Grammar of English* by R. Quirk and S. Greenbaum; HarperCollins Publishers Limited for an extract from *Collins Cobuild English Grammar*; the *Plymouth Evening Herald*; the *Plympton, Plymstock and Ivybridge News*; the Exeter *Express and Echo*; Penguin Books Ltd and Aitken, Stone and Wylie Ltd for the extract from 'On cannibal farm' from *Beyond the Dragon's Mouth* by Shiva Naipaul (Hamish Hamilton, 1984) © Shiva Naipaul, 1984. Reproduced in the British Commonwealth including Canada by permission of Hamish Hamilton Ltd, reproduced in the rest of the world by permission of Aitken, Stone and Wylie Ltd; and Aitken, Stone and Wylie for the extract from *The Middle Passage* by V. S. Naipaul.

Every effort has been made to trace copyright holders of material produced in this book. Any rights not acknowledged here will be acknowledged in subsequent printings if notice is given to the publisher.

INTRODUCTION

Awareness-raising about English is the main purpose of this book. We might actually talk about 'awareness' – readers can become aware of their own attitudes towards English *and* the use of language in society in more general terms, for example. They can also become more aware of the way in which English 'works': its systems and organization. Alternatively, one can become more aware of how users draw upon the systems of English to create meaning. Language may be regarded both as a means to a social end and as an object of study in itself.

Studying the system

Careful study of how language works, the rule-governed systems that it utilizes and realizes (and the seemingly inevitable exceptions to these rules) will repay the reader with insights into the systems of the language and its use by speakers and writers. As I write these words now, for instance, I am consciously aware that I am weighing up my options – for example, grammatically, lexically and in the way that I am structuring my message. I want you, the reader, to understand what I am trying to say, and I am using the system to try to create the best possible message. There is no guarantee I will succeed. Choosing from the multitude of choices I am faced with as a writer is not normally a conscious matter, although being more consciously aware of what we do with language might be an advantage. (I could have written 'with which I am faced . . .', for example, or said 'confronted' instead of 'faced with', but I have decided to be slightly 'informal' in this introduction. I do not want to frighten you off with a string of jargon-ridden sentences which do not appear to end.) The aim of many of the activities in this book is to make explicit to the reader some of the unconscious processes which we tap into when using English. While insights into the system of English may not lead to your becoming a better speaker or writer of English as such, they may assist you in understanding English, or teaching English better, if you are or wish to become a teacher. In an era when information is such a valuable commodity, and when so much is carried by language, we need to be in control of language, to understand its subtleties – the nature of the medium as well as the messages it carries.

Explicit knowledge

Explicit knowledge of grammar or lexical use is not a particularly fashionable type of knowledge in some circles. However, the exercises and activities in this book are designed to explore explicit knowledge and unconscious processes, too. By exploring these processes, the user might make them explicit. This is not a new activity as such – linguists have been doing this for several generations past. This book approaches the topic from a different perspective, in which the activities are a question of participation and exploration. The activities will not necessarily provide you with instant answers to questions of grammar or lexical use, however. The aim is not directly to expand our knowledge of language. (There is already in existence a copious literature on language – the 'Further reading' section is provided to enable readers to follow up and extend their knowledge of English.)

My aim is to provoke thought and reflection on English. If you use English as part of your everyday life in society, or regularly in your work, for example, it is not my place in this book to tell you how to do this 'properly' – how you use language is your choice. You may want to be more accurate or more subtle – the activities might help you in this. There are many unknowns and pitfalls in language use. Many of these are recorded somewhere in the literature on language. Through these activities, readers can reaffirm or uncover these truths and unknowns for themselves.

Aspects of English

I have not attempted to cover every aspect of English in the book. Rather, I have chosen to focus on some of the most problematic areas in English. These have been chosen on the basis of my teaching experience with speakers of other languages attempting to learn English. The insights of non-native speakers can provide both native speakers and other non-native speaker learners with cause to reflect on various aspects of English. If you are a non-native speaker of English, fresh perspectives may help you to gain greater insight into English, and, it is hoped, greater control over its use. Above all, if you are involved in any aspect of language in education, the exercises are designed to assist you in deepening insights about English, and to make connections between knowledge *about* the system of English and knowledge of *how* English is used and learned, and thus to how it might be taught. Teachers of English need to know how the language works as well as what it can achieve (just as we would not expect a teacher of physics to enter class without a knowledge of the subject, or send an innumerate maths teacher to class, neither should the language teacher enter class ignorant). By engaging oneself with English, the reader/user of this book will address the question of system use in creative and challenging means.

How to use this book

As I have said, this book does not provide answers as such. The 'answers' will emerge from your exploration of the data samples, from the tasks and from discussion with each other as you do the activities.

Each chapter of the book addresses a different topic. You are invited to do the activities in each chapter in the sequence suggested by the book. This sequence is designed to take you from your present state of knowledge to new insights, and potentially to a revised stance on a variety of language points and issues. The processes of comparing, guessing, classifying and so on that the activities will encourage should enable you to sharpen your linguistic tools and to think and reflect actively about English and language in general.

In each main section of the book, the following types of material are provided

1) Activities working on specific aspects of language data or readers' attitudes and ideas about language. These are designed to involve you in a question about language or a problematic sample of language. These activities may enable you to generate rules, or make statements about English, for example.
2) Thinking questions, which invite you to *reflect* on the insights and experiences that the previous activities have raised.
3) Further ideas; short sections – part commentary, part thought-provoking – which may stimulate you to develop your ideas about the topic under scrutiny.
4) Tasks, which enable you to investigate language on your own or to see how language is used in authentic sources. They invite you to collect and classify data, and to work with informants to interpret and understand the data.

Note: An asterisk marks an erroneous or incorrect utterance.

You can enter the content sequence at any point, and work within any activity set on any tasks that you think are particularly useful. You may of course find that working from general attitudes towards language through the consideration and analysis of specific language points enables you to develop your thinking in particular ways. Knowing about language is not only a question of knowledge – it is also a matter of attitude/judgement/value. Insights into your own attitudes towards language, for example, can help you deepen your knowledge about language, in particular the nature of the choices between alternatives that speakers make. Whichever way you choose to work, you will be challenged to become committed to thinking about language and refining your judgements. Some of these judgements may remain as questions – if they are new questions, then the activities have succeeded in their purpose.

In addition to the activities which involve you in analysis, there are further activities which may involve leaps of the imagination, intuitive judgement, and the use of all the senses. These exercises may not suit your particular way of thinking or working; you are, however, invited to try them out and are urged to reserve judgement until you have. The exercises are designed to 'loosen' your thinking – you may develop new insights as a result. Studying language can be both creative and fun!

To tutors

If you are using this book with a group of students, either as a 'course' or as a supplementary source of material, you will most probably want to use it to enhance your favoured teaching style. A few points might help you do this to maximum benefit:

1) The activities have been designed with no specific time limits in mind. Different groups and individuals will work more or less quickly, and more or less deeply on the activities. Allow plenty of time for students to respond to tasks and for them to give feedback following discussion. You can encourage the interaction between group members by, for example, asking small groups to produce composite responses to tasks and to circulate these to group members for comments and further questions to clarify what has been written. Alternatively, you could invite students to make poster displays of main points emerging from activities for future reference by the group. Another way of getting students to 'store' insights is to ask them to compile a 'mini-grammar' of rules they discover.

2) Allow students ample time for reflection following activities. Students need the opportunity to evaluate experiences, to decide what they have learned, to express doubts and to clarify certain points. Reflection can be assisted by asking students to focus on specific issues, in a structured discussion framework.

3) Ensure there are resources for students to use – reference grammars, etc. In Chapter 1 there is an exercise which you may wish to use to help students make a choice of reference grammar.

4) Do not be tempted to spoon feed the students – the exercises are designed for them to explore. The answers to all the exercises are to be found somewhere in reference grammars and dictionaries – it is desirable that students should practise using these sources. Join in discussions by all means, and make sure you know about a point, but also be prepared to reserve judgement on an issue. The tutor's basic role in these activities is to help students develop insights into English.

Learning about language can be challenging, intellectually stimulating and enjoyable. I hope these activities help you to achieve these goals.

1

LANGUAGE AND YOU

Introduction

This part of the book explores your ideas about language, your attitudes towards language and its use by different speakers and writers, and the implications of these ideas and attitudes for the ways in which you might study language and teach and learn language.

In the course of our explorations, we shall encounter the views of other users of English, grammarians and professional linguists and language teachers. These views will enable you to develop your own ideas about language, and to ask yourself relevant questions about English and its use both in the world at large and in the classroom. The views of the professionals cannot be read as 'answers', however. They are intended as an aid to your own development as a language user and analyst. Ultimately, the most satisfying and relevant 'answers' will be ones you have developed and internalized.

This section also invites you to explore your own attitudes and beliefs about language in a number of ways. In order to make sense of these explorations, it is important that you spend as long as possible on the 'thinking questions' and opportunities for reflection which follow activities in the text. It is hoped that the practice of pausing to reflect on what we have done will enable us to maximize the benefits of activity and experience.

One very valuable way of making sense of your encounters with language both while using this book and in your daily life will be to keep a record of these encounters in a diary or journal (or similar), in which you record unusual or striking instances of language use, your thoughts on language or your experiences of doing the activities in this book. Regular review of your journal will provide raw material for language work, and will also help in establishing patterns in your own thinking about language.

What is your image of language?

Aim To explore our images and 'hidden knowledge' about language through the images.

ACTIVITY 1.1

What do you see?

There are many ways in which we could describe language. We could, for instance, liken language to an *ocean* – it is never still, it has many moods and shapes, it carries people and their goods, it seems to be endless . . . perhaps you could add to this list.

Write down a few more ways in which you think language might be like an ocean. Share these ideas with a colleague, classmate or friend.

What do *you* compare a language with? Note your response. (Make a simple sketch or drawing of your image if you wish.) Then write down all the ways in which language reflects the image you see.

Share your image with a colleague, classmate or friend:

- Note features of your images which you have in common.
- Note significant differences between your images.

ACTIVITY 1.2

What are we using?

We are all users of language. Social life would be impossible without language; once we have learnt to understand and speak our native tongue (L1), we use it for a bewildering variety of purposes. We also develop and refine our use of our L1 as we grow up and pass through stages and experiences in our lives. An important process for most of us is our encounter with the written word as we gradually learn to become literate. The skills and abilities associated with literacy extend our range as language users.

Think about using a language, either your own or a foreign language – whether listening to, speaking, reading or writing the language. What, precisely, are you using when you use language? What does language consist of? Write down as many components of language as you can (for example, words, sounds, etc.). Share these with a friend, colleague or classmate. Discuss each other's lists and extend your own.

Thinking questions

1) Is English your friend or foe? Can you explain why?
2) Look back at your image in Activity 1.1 and the components you have listed in Activity 1.2. Which parts of language do you like? Which parts are your 'friends'? Which parts don't you like? Which parts are your 'foes'? Can you say why you look at language in this particular way?
3) Have you found out anything new about your ideas on language from doing these activities?

4) Did you find it easy/comfortable/exciting (or any other way of describing it) while working on your image of language? Or did you find it easier thinking about components of language? Which was the most productive for you?

Further ideas

In order to help you clarify and develop your ideas on language and what it consists of, and the way in which you 'see' it, read the following short text:

> Our images of language will have been shaped by a number of influences and experiences. These will include any or all of the following:
>
> - Informal experiences as children 'playing' with language and testing out its powers and potential. For most children, language seems infinitely flexible and fun. Is language still like that for you? Or is it a more serious business these days?
> - Formal experiences of learning languages, either mother tongue or foreign languages. The ways in which language is treated by teachers and textbooks can influence the ways in which we view language. Were you exposed to a 'nuts and bolts' view – that language was a system to be assembled? Or was it treated as a rich, diverse and unpredictable system for expressing your innermost thoughts and feelings? Or both of these? Or something else?
> - The attention and importance our families and peer groups gave to language as we grew up, and the attitudes those near us held (and hold) about language and its use. For example, many parents insist that their children should 'speak properly'.
> - The literature, such as novels, poems, etc., we have read and currently read. The language to which we are exposed influences us in many hidden ways, from the occurrence of new vocabulary to the organization of messages in longer texts.
> - Newspapers, magazines and other print media with which we have regular encounters. 'Contemporary' language use is mirrored in these sources.

Ultimately, whatever influences we have been open to, we could divide our views of language into two broad groups, which describe two broad tendencies. The first set are *holistic* views, which portray language as a unified entity. This view is the user's view, 'speaking naturally', the intuitive use of language without conscious consideration of its organization and structure. Language is a tool to be used.

The second set are *analytical* views which see language as a series of interlocking components. This is a systematic view. Immediately we stop to think about language and how it works, and whether or not it has elements distinguishable one from another, we start to become analytical. Developing the analytical faculty could be described as 'sharpening the language tool', although there is some dispute as to whether being aware of the system leads to more precise use.

In essence, there is truth in both the holistic and analytical tendencies; they merely approach language from different viewpoints, mirroring the ways in which their proponents either view the world, or their purposes for looking at language as an object of contemplation, interest, study or investigation. What we have here is a continuum of tendencies: we tend to 'lean' towards holistic or analytical views of language, often influenced by the circumstances in which we are thinking or acting. Users of language are sensitive to language use in many ways, and it is best to see the analytical view as a refinement of this sensitivity.

To pursue the simple analogy of language as an ocean, on a map of the world, or a photograph taken from space, the ocean is a blue, untroubled mass. However, it *does* certain things (it has powers); it *is* certain things (it has attributes). It is the ocean, seamless and apparently uniform. On the other hand, it is composed of a multitude of elements; it contains many life forms; it has its own internal circulation patterns and more. We humans have also divided it up into named parts, for our convenience, despite its continuity around the land mass of the globe.

All these views and facts are true – but only part of the whole truth. However, we tend to prefer one tendency to the other. We seem to be, by nature, either holists or analysts. Which do you think you are? What evidence do you have for this view? Our images of what we see and know in the world will undoubtedly reflect these tendencies. However, for the full picture we need to see in both ways.

TASKS

Decide on whether or not the views expressed in the quotations below are essentially holistic or analytical, or contain elements of both tendencies.

1) Rewrite or paraphrase each quotation so that it expresses the idea in your own terms.
2) Decide on the implications of each for the student of language. Which one do you think would be the most challenging for you as a student?

A. Language is as it is because of the functions it has evolved to serve (Halliday, 1970, in Kress, 1976: 26).

B. ... communication cannot be studied in isolation; it must be analysed in terms of its effect on people's lives. We must focus on what communication does: how it constrains evaluation and decision-making, not merely how it is structured (Gumperz, 1982:1).

C. ... any sentence of the language may be represented as a particular arrangement of ... the minimal grammatical elements of which it is composed (Lyons, 1968: 115).

Talking about language

Aim To examine ways in which speakers of English talk about the language and the ways in which people use it.

We are all in the habit of talking about language and of describing ways in which people use language. All languages have a rich variety of expressions that help us do this. This activity, in several parts, is designed to explore some of the 'language about language' used in English.

Pretask
Consider what the expression 'a way with words' means in the context of 'He or she's got a way with words'. What social, intellectual and personal attributes are we describing? Are there other language user's attributes which this expression describes?

ACTIVITY 1.3

A)   What does each of these expressions tell you about language or our attitudes towards language and its users? (Use a dictionary if you are unfamiliar with these expressions.)

1) He doesn't *speak our language*.
2) Many people hate *bad language*.
3) He used very *strong language*.
4) She used *plain language*.
5) He didn't *mince his words*.
6) She's rather *mealy mouthed* about some things.
7) She can't stop *hedging*.

B)   What do the following terms mean with reference to people's use of language?

waffle   mumbo-jumbo   gibberish   slang   jargon   silver-tongued
banter   to talk someone round   to talk yourself out of something
the gift of the gab   to mouth obscenities at people   gobbledegook
a cutting remark   to sweet talk   double talk   Newspeak
chat up   talk posh   sound bite

Which ones are positive and which are negative?

TASKS

1)   Make a list of as many expressions as you can which are constructed with the verbs *speak* or *say* (e.g., 'speak one's mind'). Use reference books, ask informants or use any other way you can think of to build up your list of expressions.
2)   Collect as many expressions as possible which might be described as slang or jargon. Note the context – occupation or social grouping, for example – in which the jargon occurs (e.g., many sports have a jargon).

Thinking questions
1)   What does our language about language as others and ourselves use it tell us about the basis of many of our beliefs and attitudes about language?
2)   Are we ever neutral – nonjudgemental – when we talk about our own and others' use of language? Comment.

ACTIVITY 1.4

Examine the list of verbs that follows. They are all used to refer to ways of speaking. Read through the list of verbs and complete a table as shown below by asking yourself the following questions:

● Which words are *neutral*? Referring only to the *activity* of speaking?
● Which describe *loud* speech?
● Which describe *soft* or *quiet* speech?
● Which describe either *rapid* or *slow* speech?
● Which describe something in the *tone* of the speaker's voice?
● Which require the listener to *act* on the basis of what they hear?
● Which *evaluate* the speaker in some way?

---

call   threaten   talk   ask   insist   scold   whisper   request
appeal   pray   shout   gabble   discuss   argue   mumble   demand
remind   beg   lecture   warn   scream   mutter   yell   babble
suggest   splutter   intone   query   enquire   chat
chatter   remark

Neutral	Loud	Soft	Rapid	Slow	Tonal	Listener acts	Evaluate
Call	*Call*				*Call*	*Call*	

Thinking questions
1) Look back over the various parts of this activity. What have you learned about the ways in which users of a language express their attitudes and ideas about both the language and the ways in which it is used?
2) What do you think are the possible implications of what you have discovered in these activities for
   a) teachers of language (either mother tongue or foreign language or both);
   b) learners of language (either mother tongue or foreign language);
   c) your own use of English (as native or non-native speaker); and
   d) language in social relationships?

Further ideas

A)   As users of English, we are inevitably predisposed towards making judgements and statements about language in general, specific uses or users of language in general, and about English, in particular. The basis of these statements and judgements lies in our *communicative competence* (Canale (1983), for example). As speakers of a language, we have an underlying knowledge of how the language is structured, how it is used in connected discourse, how it can be used in different ways in different social circumstances, and how we can use a language strategically, either to get our way, for example, or to repair fences. Communicative competence is an amalgam of intuition, knowledge, strategy and sensitivity built on experience in different social and psychological settings. In this complex lie our attitudes, values and beliefs – thus, when we judge a speaker's use of language, our attitudes are 'activated'.

B)   Attitudes and beliefs lie at the subjective, emotional, even prejudiced end of the subjective objective continuum. Most of our statements about language are subjective ('I don't like the way he speaks . . .'). It is where these judgements begin to overlap with a more objective knowledge of, say, grammar, that the territory of the linguist – interested in structure, form and competence

(Chomsky (1957)) is entered. Linguists claim dispassionate, 'scientific' knowledge. And yet who is the best judge of who is 'speaking proper'? The linguist or the lay person?

C)   Sociolinguistics – contextually-based language study – has attempted to move cautiously into the world of the real user, the lay person. Sociolinguistics is interested in attitudes to language, how speakers react to different varieties, the nature of different varieties, and so on. By moving into this territory, sociolinguists invariably encounter value systems, issues related to culture and class and so on. In for example, Edwards (1976) and Gumperz (1982) an attempt has been made to describe and account for these aspects of language use. Ultimately, it seems that language use is influenced by speakers' and hearers' intentions, motivations and attitudes – the affective domain. The study of sociolinguistics thus offers an important 'window' into previously hidden areas of communicative competence, such as attitude and value.

From form-based studies of language we have developed a sophisticated range of analytical tools for describing language. This has enabled us to objectify our judgements more clearly. The metalanguage – language about language – enables us to do the following:

1)   Identify and describe different elements or parts of language (noun, phrase, etc.).
2)   Discuss relationships between these elements and the rules and conventions that govern these relationships (linkers, discourse).
3)   Describe functions of language (narrative, etc.).

Metalanguage is rarely used in everyday speech, unless some form of criticism or evaluation is implied. We rarely hear someone talking about 'modal verbs' unless they are analysing someone's use of language in specific professional settings, as in mother tongue or foreign language teaching. It is in this latter context that metalanguage is employed for descriptive or analytically value-free purposes. It can help the student of a foreign language understand aspects of the language and share them in an unambiguous way with others familiar with the terminology.

Our 'language about language' is evidence of our ability to stand back from an everyday human activity. This means of describing, interpreting and trying to reach an understanding of what we do with language is a priceless asset. Its systematic application in language study is an extension of this natural tendency of speakers to describe and judge others' use of language.

Thinking questions

Note your reactions to the metalanguage issue. How often, for example, do you find yourself resorting to use of some type of metalanguage when talking about someone's use of language? How often do you find yourself passing judgement on a speaker (e.g. 'He's a waffler')? What *social* factors do you think influence our judgements about language and language use?

1)   Make a list of nouns and adjectives people use to identify types of language, e.g., jargon, waffle, etc. List them in positive, negative and neutral categories.
2)   Find some English-speaking informants and ask for their reactions to the different words you have listed in 1) above – do they see the words in the same ways as you (positively etc.)? Do they regularly use these words? Are there any others they use?

Territory to explore

Aim   To examine our attitudes and ideas about learning English and other languages.

Explorers rarely set off on a journey without a map of some kind, even if it is simple or rudimentary. Even if they go to what is to them new territory, they will probably have some idea about what to find or expect. These sources are usually reports from previous travellers, legends and myths, and peers and friends with opinions and ideas.

- Where does your knowledge of English originate?
- Is it from previous explorers, myths and legends?
- Is it influenced by the opinions of your friends, your newspaper or your family?

Think about beginning an exploration of English

What is your map of English like at the moment? What are the main features in the territory? What are the obstacles and dangers for travellers in this territory? What are the pleasant places, or places you feel at home in? Are there places you know nothing about?

1)   List all the main features of English that you think should be on *your* explorer's map.
2)   Draw a map to guide a new explorer in this territory, so that the person can find the features that you are familiar with. The map can be as stylized and 'imaginary' as you want. The simple map of 'Maths territory' (Figure 1.1) might provide you with some inspiration.

FIG. 1.1   Maths territory.

Thinking questions

1) Do you think there is any set 'route' a traveller should follow through your English territory? If so, can you plot it at this stage? Do you think we can explore any language according to a set route?

2) What 'equipment' would you take with you, or advise, for an explorer in this territory? In what ways could they be useful to the explorer? (The maths explorer might take a calculator, logarithm tables, a protractor and an abacus, among other things.)

3) You might like to reflect on the potential benefits of exploring 'English territory'. How could an exploration of English benefit you? If you are a native speaker, are there aspects of your language with which you are unfamiliar? If you are a non-native speaker, could you benefit from deepening, or clarifying your knowledge of English in any way?

If you have done this activity at the beginning of your explorations, it would be useful to keep your map and refer to it from time to time. As you become familiar with the territory, you might like to alter or update the map, as explorers always do.

You might also want to keep a 'log' of your explorations, so that the route and the obstacles and successes you encountered on your way can be a source of review and reflection at a later date.

Further ideas

The territory of language has been explored many times and by many different people over the years. One of the most famous of the recent 'explorers' is Noam Chomsky. English itself has been explored on numerous occasions; as you read this, there will be explorers out in that territory.

There are many different maps in existence. It is hardly surprising that the map has been continually redrawn by successive explorers, though. At various times in history, the territory looked different from what it does today – the explorer of Shakespeare's English would certainly not find modern British English completely familiar, for example. The landscape has eroded gradually over the centuries. New life-forms have established themselves as the language has changed and evolved. Occasionally there have been events equivalent to a linguistic earthquake, like the emergence of North America as a homeland of English. The results of the explorations have also depended to some extent on the instruments they have used (telescope or magnifying glass? sketchbook or camera? notebook or computer?) and to a great extent on what the explorers believe the territory to be like – their preconceptions. This, in turn, will depend on the explorer's tendencies to see the whole, the parts or the sum of the parts in language (see 'What is your image of language?', above). Finally, the language which they use, and the names they give to territory, are significant. Local inhabitants call the place Mosie-A-Tunya; Anglophones call it Victoria Falls: 'The Smoke that Thunders' or a waterfall named after a Queen of England. The differences in naming can have important social and political connotations.

Explorers have returned from their travels with different stories and different maps of what is apparently the same place. For example:

- On some maps, there seems to be no human settlement, only physical elements, and the relationships between them.
- On some maps, certain areas appear in great detail, while the rest of the territory is only lightly pencilled in, or left empty.
- On some maps, the explorer's route appears.
- Maps use different symbols for the same features.
- Some maps are very interim: exploration is still proceeding.
- Some maps are projections, emphasizing some areas at the expense of others.

Some maps are essentially 'cultural', and trace the relationships between users of language and their cultures. Other maps are unashamedly 'physical', and identify and delineate the main physical features of the territory. Another approach to the exploration is to acknowledge the general accuracy of these two maps, the cultural and the physical, and to overlay one with the other, thus creating a composite map. What do you think the effect will be of such a procedure? Can you think of other types of 'language maps' which could be overlaid in this way, and the effects of the overlays (e.g., 'geological' types of map which show the juxtaposition of the different components and speculate on their origin)?

Another feature of contemporary exploration is the use of technological tools such as video, audio-tape and the computer as instruments of exploration. However, these instruments will bend to the uses to which they are put. Ultimately, what the explorer believes is 'there' will influence the use to which even the most sophisticated instrument of exploration, data storage and analysis will be put.

TASKS

1) Examine the quotes which follow, and see if you can identify the tools, the overall views of language and the types of information that the explorers have been working with in their explorations.

   A. ... language, action and knowledge are inseparable (Stubbs, 1983:1).

   B. ... we often know what kind of language to expect in different situations: and, conversely, given a fragment of language we can often reconstruct in some detail the social situation which produced it (Stubbs, 1983:2).

   C. ... grammar is based on the notion of choice. The speaker of a language, like a person engaging in any kind of culturally determined behaviour, can be regarded as carrying out, simultaneously and successively, a number of distinct choices. At any given moment, in the environment of the selections made up to that time, a certain range of further choices is available. It is the system that formalizes the notion of choice in language (Halliday, in Kress, 1976:3).

   D. ... the social and political conditions of modern life favour the creation of new linguistic symbols which can serve as the rallying point for interest group sharing.
      ... social identity and ethnicity are in large part established and maintained through language (Gumperz, 1982:7).

   E. ... it is now possible to study the problem of rule-governed creativity in natural language, the problem of constructing grammars that explicitly generate deep and surface structures and express the relations between them (Chomsky, 1957, in Allen and van Buren, 1971:5).

2) Go to your library and try to locate any books and/or journals or reference works which might help you in your explorations of English. Keep a record of what you find. Note the ways in which you think these tools could be useful.

Characteristics of language

Aim To examine your ideas about the way in which language is composed, and to add detail to what you found out in the previous sections. In this section, through the activity and follow-up exercises, we shall encounter the overlap of beliefs and knowledge about language, as held by any individual.

ACTIVITY 1.5

Which of the following statements about language do you find most convincing? Grade the statements from 1 to 5, according to how convincing you find the statement: 1 for totally unconvincing and 5 for completely convincing.

1) Language is a series of closed, unchanging systems.
2) 'Language' is too narrow a term to describe the infinite variety of codes, both verbal and nonverbal, which speakers use.
3) Language is essentially a medium of communication. The message is more important than the form.
4) Languages vary in their regularity: some languages are very regular, whereas others are very irregular (like English, for example).
5) Language is changing too quickly to make any realistic judgements about its nature.
6) Spoken language is a less than perfect form of written language.
7) A language closely reflects the culture of the people who speak it.

Thinking questions
1) What are the implications of each of the statements above for the following groups of users? For example, are there some issues that are more important for some groups than others?

   - Teachers of English as mother tongue.
   - Teachers of English as a foreign language.
   - Language policy-makers.
   - Learners of English as mother tongue (in school or other formal settings).
   - Learners of English as a foreign language.
   - Novelists, poets, etc.
   - Writers of advertising copy.

2) Do you sympathize with the view that there is a system or series of systems in any language, which constitute its essence, or basis? Furthermore, do you believe that these systems are more or less fixed? Or do you hold the view that the systems are in existence for speakers and users to exploit as they need, and that it is the users of a language who ultimately decide on the conventions for its use?

Further ideas

Read the following extracts from descriptions of English and, as you read, try to identify the author's stance on the main characteristics of English. Note, in particular, any 'technical terminology' which you think is useful, or which you find difficult to understand.

A. It is the class that enters into relations of structure and of system in language. A structure is an ordered arrangement of elements in chain relation, such as the English clause structure 'predicator + complement' (e.g., *fetch the ink*). While (in this instance) the ultimate exponent of the element 'predicator' is *fetch* and that of the element 'complement' is *the ink*, the direct exponents of these elements are respectively the class 'verbal group' and the class 'nominal group'. Similarly: a system is a limited ('closed') set of terms in choice relation, such as the English system of 'number' (e.g., *boy/boys*). While (in this instance) the ultimate exponents of the terms in the system are *boy* and *boys*, the direct exponents of these terms are the class 'singular nominal group' and the class 'plural nominal group'. It is useful to be able to distinguish classes derived in these two ways: they can be referred to respectively as 'chain classes' (those relating to structure) and 'choice classes' (those relating to system) (Halliday, 1970, in Kress, 1976:84).

B. If we were to ask a non-linguist what are the ultimate units of language, the building-blocks, so to speak, out of which utterances are constructed, he might well reply that the ultimate units of language are 'sounds' and 'words'. He might add that words are made up of sequences of sounds, each sound being represented, ideally, by a particular letter of the alphabet (in the case of languages customarily represented by a system of alphabetic writing); and that, whereas the words of a language have a meaning, the sounds do not (their sole function being to form words). These several propositions underlie the traditional view of language reflected in most grammars and dictionaries: the grammar gives rules for the construction of sentences out of words, and the dictionary tells us what the individual words mean (Lyons, 1968:53).

C. Traditional grammars make use of a fairly wide technical vocabulary to describe the concepts they use – words like 'noun', 'verb', 'agreement', 'plural', 'clause' and even 'word' itself. Some of the terms are probably unintelligible to most people, though they may have some dim recollection of them from their schooldays. Others would be more familiar – most people would know, or think they know, what is meant by 'plural' or 'noun' and everyone, I suspect, would be convinced that he knew what a word was. However, we cannot take even this for granted. We must look at both the familiar and the less familiar terms to see precisely how they are used and to ask whether their use is really justified. Unfortunately, the usual practice in the grammar is to give some kind of definition of most of the words, but never to question the whole justification of their use (Palmer, 1990:41).

TASK

Interview at least five informants to find out their views about language and its characteristics. Use the statements from Activity 1.5 to elicit their opinions, or make up a series of questions based on the statements.

What sorts of views do the informants have? Can you classify them? How far are you personally able to agree with or relate to the informants' views?

What do you think about English?

Aim   To enable readers to clarify their attitudes towards English and its users, and to begin to examine the values that influence those attitudes and beliefs.

ACTIVITY 1.6

Please read through the series of statements which follow; each one expresses people's views about English and its use. They are neither correct nor incorrect. However, you will find yourself reacting to them in one way or another, either positively or negatively. If you agree more than you disagree about a statement, put a *tick* beside it. If you disagree more than you agree, put a *cross* beside it. Please respond to *all* the statements. Be prepared to discuss your views.

1) Non-native forms of English (for example, 'Indian English', 'Malaysian English' or 'Kenyan English') are just as valid as native forms of English as, for example, British English.

2) It is best to see a language like English as a series of 'varieties'. This captures its widespread use by different national and social groups.

3) English is a hybrid language (originating from many different sources), which is currently absorbing many new influences. As such it could never have a 'correct' or 'authorized' version.

4) The practice of, for example, the 'Académie Française', which makes sure that French is kept free of foreign interference, should be extended to other languages and, in particular, English.

5) English is a language which seems infinitely flexible in terms of accents, grammatical correctness, vocabulary and so on.

6) In order to speak good English, we should study the great works of literature, e.g., Shakespeare, Dickens, etc.

7) There are clear standards of correctness and appropriateness for the use of English in, for example, BBC or 'Oxford' English.

8) English is the most important language in the world for a variety of reasons, most of them related to information storage and transfer.
9) Because English is used so widely, it is bound to be misused.
10) The present habit of making up new words like 'deplane' (to leave an aeroplane) is a blight on the English language and should be discouraged.

Thinking questions

1) List the main themes to emerge from the questionnaire above in terms of language use. Express these as a set of *key words* which can be drawn from the statements above, for example, 'standards' in 7).
2) What, for you, is the main issue to be raised by the questionnaire?
   Does your being either a native or a non-native speaker of English seem to influence your views? What do you think the other's viewpoint might be?

ACTIVITY 1.7

Write a reply to the letter below, stating your position with regard to 'Americanisms' in English.

Proper English

What a pity it is that a member of your editorial staff devised the headline that he did to caption the letter from Mr Bert Thomas (Herald,
5 January 3). I refer, of course, to 'No hassle on Sundays', in which a ghastly Americanism was substituted for the adequately descriptive word 'bother'.

I am saddened to see that your
10 otherwise excellent newspaper is thus subscribing to the erosion of proper English.

Donald W. Major
(*Plymouth Evening Herald*,
9 January 1992).

ACTIVITY 1.8

Read the article below and respond to the questions on specific points in it.

English as she is mis-spoke

Funny old language, ain't it?

Sorry, Esperanto. It was a brave notion to invent a universal language, and the world some day may have one – Mandarin? Martian? 5 Microcircuitous? – but for the time being it makes do with English. Which English, and for what time being? Some sensible teachers of English fear that the time will not be long if some 10 other teachers are not more rigorous about the English they teach.

These others draw their attitudes from the anything-goes 1960s. Forget Oxford English, it was argued. If kids 15 talk Geordie or Jamaican, or their American parallels, at home, teach them to express themselves in the dialect they know. That argument spread with the arrival in Britain of Asians, 20 in America of Hispanics, whose home life was not conducted in any kind of English. Should they be taught standard English, or that of the neighbourhood where they had settled? The 25 British at the time were abandoning the belief, which Americans had never held, that there was only one correct accent. If accents could vary, why not accept every variety of English?

30 The weakness of such arguments was cruelly exposed in Britain in the 1980s: to rap in Rastafarian may be a liberating skill, but it is not one that many employers want to hire. 35 Few teachers today would argue that there is only one correct variety of English; some English has to be translated into American to avoid technical misunderstandings. But fewer still 40 argue that simply anything goes. Nor do many West Indian or Hispanic parents thank those who do.

For 'parents' read 'governments',

and you have the argument in its 45 international form. Native teachers of English in, say, Japan normally aim to teach standard English, whether in its British or American variety. That is what Japanese employers expect. They 50 are increasingly miffed when British or American teachers imported to guide them in this task express doubts whether it is worth attempting.

Colaba side needs cleaning up

The imported teachers say there is 55 a long-established variant of English used in India. If British or American English, why not Indian English or Japanese English? Why try to draw any line? In the homelands of Eng-60 lish, jargon is rife, and not only among scientists and brasshats. Literary critics cheerfully write a dense deconstructionist gibberish. Are they using their native tongue any better 65 than someone who says, 'You is, ain't you'? Some Indians use a courtly English almost forgotten in its own land; others will say 'You are staying Colaba side, isn't it?' – to English ears 70 an odd way of asking whether one lives in that part of Bombay, yet intelligible from one end of India to the other. Is English grammar supposed to kick out such phrases, while its databanks 75 accession Haigspeak?

It is now clear that the answer, even from India, is yes. The English that such countries want is one that enables Indians to communicate not 80 just with each other, but with the English-speaking world. Thank you for your tolerance, they say, but we'd prefer your standard English (*The Economist*, 16 July 1988:18).

Questions

1) In paragraph 1, what do you think is meant by 'rigorous about the English they teach'?
2) In paragraph 2 it is claimed that certain attitudes prevailed in the 1960s. What were these attitudes and what were the outcomes: (a) in Britain; and (b) in the USA? What social forces led to these events? Why was it easier for the Americans to absorb any changes in attitude?
3) In paragraph 3, the article identifies certain outcomes of the 1960s' attitudes in the 1980s; what were these?
4) What is the 'Japanese attitude' towards English (paragraph 4)?
5) What is the main theme of the questions asked in paragraph 5?
6) What sorts of standard is the article advocating?

Make a list of the claims the article makes. What is your response to each of the article's claims? Do you agree or disagree with each of the claims? Do you find you need more information in order to respond to the claims?

Thinking questions

What are your views now on the idea of 'standards' of language use? Do you think it is important to have a clear line on 'standards' of language use?

Further ideas

Received pronunciation (RP) and standard English

Arguments about the relative merits and demerits of trying to define a 'standard' form of English are not a new phenomenon in 'educated' circles in England. The arguments have been strongly influenced by the rapid growth in the twentieth century of mass media all over the world. Before the availability of radio and television, and mass travel and migration within Britain, there was no real worry about what was a 'standard' form of English. Educated people had a broad consensus about standard English, satirized by Shaw's *Pygmalion*. It was certainly no accident that the prevalent accent on the airwaves in the early days of the BBC was the accent of its controllers and the royal family, and the intellectual and political élite. And yet it has been estimated that today as little as 3% of the British population regularly use the RP variety of English (McCrum, Cran and McNeil, 1986). Many others are exposed to RP or near-RP in their education. They may or may not adopt it as their variety. And yet when there are discussions of standards and acceptability in English, RP remains the yardstick for many. A further factor from descriptive linguistics was the work of Daniel Jones (1959) in producing the first fully authorized description of the phonetic structure of English. He described RP; if we open an English dictionary today to find the proposed pronunciation of a word, we will find the RP version. There is though a clear distinction to be made between RP descriptions and what people do with language. Is the question of a standard a red herring?

Cultural identity

In the international context, it is very important that most non-native speakers who have learnt English have been at some time exposed to the RP variety. Most non-native speakers do not speak the variety, but there is often an unconscious desire among non-native speakers to acquire an RP accent. On the BBC World Service many newsreaders still use the RP variety – it is the voice of Britain. Some (see Phillipson, 1991) might regard this as a means of imposing a particular variety on the world, although the American variety is the most likely to be encountered worldwide for political and economic reasons as much as for cultural ones – for example, through television, cinema and the ubiquitous 'news magazine' like *Time* or *Newsweek*.

The discussion is a prelude to a further exploration of the issue of accent and identity (social and personal, cultural and national). In Britain there are a large number of accents, corresponding to different regions of the country. Some observers also relate accents to different social classes (Trudgill, 1974). The picture is complicated by the existence of regional dialects, which feature grammatical and lexical variations from the (essentially) London and Home Counties variety. Because speakers have choice, they may choose to exaggerate their regionality, nationality, social class: to 'hypercorrect' (Hughes and Trudgill, 1987). With such a range of choices, how can the standard be defined? Identity seems to have prevalence over standardization.

(Labov (1970) makes important points on the same issue, drawing on different accents from the North Eastern United States.)

Standard English

So what is the standard? What *are* standards of language use anyway? To define these in terms of descriptions which do not acknowledge change is to defy reality. (So what do you think about the grammatical sensibilities of a bus company in Britain that advertises itself under the slogan 'MORE SENSE/LESS PENCE'? Or the nearly ubiquitous glottal stop in Southern England?) To impose a standard has overtones of élitism and certainly courts arguments against regional bias. As it is, British speakers of English have to learn to understand new varieties when they come into contact with people from different occupational groups, different regions, or even the opposite gender (Tannen, 1991).

The facts seem to be as follows:

1) There is a vast variety of 'Englishes' spoken worldwide. The fact that they are recognizably English points to the existence of a possible 'core' grammar or lexicon. But the variations are vast, particularly as regards spoken English.

2) Because language is so closely bound up with social, political and cultural identity, to impose or to insist on a specific standard in language production can have serious social, political and cultural implications (Gumperz, 1982).

3) There are a great number of descriptions of English, but it is noticeable that, as professional linguists continue to study instances of real language use, descriptions have to be modified in order to accommodate the wide variations in usage (e.g., Cobuild Dictionaries and Grammars).

Let us leave this section with the views of two professional linguists who represent the opposing camps in this controversial area.

A. I do not believe that the traditional notions of codification, standardization, models and methods apply to English any more. The dichotomy of its *native* and *non-native* users seems to have become irrelevant. We may talk of 'standards for our linguistic satisfaction', but we seem to be at a loss to explain what we mean by them, and equally important, how to apply them. I do not think that in discussing standards for English, the sociolinguistic reality of each English-using speech fellowship can be ignored (Kachru, 1985:29).

B. I believe that the fashion of undermining belief in standard English has wrought educational damage in the ENL countries, though I am ready to concede that there may well have been compensating educational gains in the wider tolerance for an enjoyment of the extraordinary variety of English around us in any of these countries. But then just such an airy contempt for standards started to be exported to EFL and ESL countries, and for this I can find no such mitigating compensation. The relatively narrow range of purposes for which the non-native needs to use English is arguably well catered for by a single monochrome standard form that looks as good on paper as it sounds in speech (Quirk, 1985:6).

Which of the authors do you find yourself sympathizing with? Why? What is your view? What is the evidence?

TASKS

1) Interview at least five informants (try for a mix between native and non-native speakers if you can) and elicit their views on the attitudes expressed in Activities 1.6–1.8.

Make up a series of statements or questions of your own, based on the views you have already encountered to guide your interviews. What broad trends do you see emerging from the interviews?

2) Keep a book of cuttings from the press of articles and features on language and language use.

Correct or not?

Aim To assist the reader in understanding the types of judgement that we make about language in use. These judgements are related to our views about the correctness and the acceptability of language in use.

ACTIVITY 1.9

Look through the samples of English which follow. Make decisions on the *grammatical correctness* of each utterance. Use a 3-point scale, with 3 for completely correct, 2 for grammatically incorrect but acceptable and 1 for totally incorrect.

 1) The boy Lineker done brilliant.
 2) Mansell's done superbly well this afternoon.
 3) There was less people there than I expected.
 4) That's no great hassle.
 5) I would like to stress on this point.
 6) We're in real problems.
 7) There's more to him than what you think.
 8) We was on holiday last week.
 9) She was there I tell you.
10) A: Who did that?
    B: Me. I did it.
11) I ain't gonna do it.
12) This product has real drinkability.
13) I picked him outside the cinema and we went to his place.
14) I can't be accepting your contribution.
15) Who you looking at then?
16) The fish cooked beautifully.
17) I'm happy, aren't I?
18) She's sat down by the window.
19) Did you use to enjoy weight training?
20) You'll get hurt if you carry on.
21) We're talking really big money.
22) Travelling alone is *serious* travelling.
23) I would of gone if I'd had the money.

Note: A key for the sentences is given on p. 29.

ACTIVITY 1.10

Now give each example a similar rating for *acceptability*. Is there any discrepancy between the two scores you have given? Can you explain any discrepancy?

If you think any of the examples rate a score of 1 on either grammaticality or acceptability, can you provide a correction?

Thinking question
Do you perceive any major differences between the notions of grammaticality and acceptability? Are there any overlaps? Does the fact that people might say rather than write something influence your view? Comment.

ACTIVITY 1.11

Why do you think people object to occurrences like the following?

1) APPLE'S 10p EACH.
2) He was so hungry, that he fell over.
3) There were'nt many guests, it was a shame.
4) 'Where do you think you're going, he said?'
5) Its not as hot as I thought it would be.

Thinking questions
Is it really true to say that punctuation is unimportant? Are there links between spoken language and punctuation? If so, what are these?

ACTIVITY 1.12

Are you familiar with these words and expressions in English? What does each one mean?

movious   a go-down   on seat   a bottle store   a bioscope
download   plannification   regionalization   a mealie
to fair out   walkative

Note: A key for the words and expressions is given on p. 30.

Thinking questions
Does the development of new words in a language mean that the language is becoming degraded in any way? What does the development of new words tell us about language?

Further ideas

Language change

Why do languages change? In what ways do they change? Is it possible to standardize a language like English?

In the present-day pluralistic world of mass media and travel, in which English is the dominant language of communication, the questions of language change and 'standards' have become important, often emotionally-charged issues. Linguists and sociolinguists have long been fascinated by the shifting, variable nature of languages over time. They have identified specific areas of language which change.

a) *The Lexicon* is the most volatile element of any language. In an era of new inventions, new ways of perceiving the world and new ways of expressing ourselves, English has changed and developed to accommodate the changes. Thus we have 'motherboards' in computers, we talk about 'personal growth' and 'soft systems management' and 'glitzy' fashion. Naming and renaming are familiar actions throughout our lives as language users – we rarely pause to reflect on what is happening in English, or any other language. An example is the way in which English school children's vocabulary changes rapidly to keep up with new ideas, renaming and new fashion. English also absorbs elements of the lexicon of other languages ('jamboree' and 'palaver'). The meanings of items shift and change over the years, too – you might like to consider specific items of English vocabulary which have changed meaning in this way.

b) *The Grammatical System* changes much more slowly than the lexicon. We can perceive differences between the grammar of Shakespeare or Milton and today, for example. English grammar appears to be being simplified by its users today, for example, the omission of primary auxiliaries, especially 'have' in some verb groups or the trend towards substituting 'less' for 'fewer' as in expressions like 'less people'. These changes are slow, however, and a speaker of English may not be aware of changes during their own lifetimes. Again, you might be interested in investigating other elements of English grammar which seem to be changing. (Listen to 'radio news' for examples.)

c) *Pronunciation* Accents come and go in terms of their popularity – in the 1960s it was, for example, popular among younger English people to affect Liverpool or South London accents in reverence of their favourite rock stars (the Beatles and Rolling Stones, among others). Currently in Britain, the glottal stop has become widespread among young speakers of English – presumably because of the influence of London accents on the television. On the other hand, RP use is comparatively rare among young British English speakers.

Pidgins and Creoles

Pidgin languages – languages with no native speakers (Holmes, 1992), and Creoles – pidgins which have acquired native speakers, are interesting examples of how new languages have developed.

a)   *Trade and Communication*   When people with differing native languages have traded or worked closely together for a long period, they have always developed ways of communicating. The history of European trade, expansionism and imperialism is, in part, a history of the development and growth of new languages or new forms of English. Creoles, for example, as spoken in Haiti (based on French) and Sierra Leone (based on English) are examples of this phenomenon. In other parts of West Africa, a pidgin is widely spoken in Ghana, Nigeria and West Cameroon. The base language of this pidgin is generally regarded as English (Todd, 1984), from which the grammar has developed. On the other hand, the lexicon is a pot pourri of English, Portuguese, French and local languages. The pidgin thus varies from country to country, depending on the relative influence of the vernacular. The pronunciation is based on local languages. Unlike many pidgins, the West African pidgins have survived and even thrived – in Nigeria, there is an established literature in pidgin and many popular songs have pidgin lyrics. An example of a pidgin that has died is the pidgin that developed for use between American troops and the Vietnamese. Another feature of pidgins is that when they coexist with groups who speak a prestigious world language like English as in Nigeria, they are generally regarded as low-status.

b)   *Non-native varieties* (NNFs)   NNFs are the final part of the great jigsaw that is the English language. In countries in East Africa, West Africa, the Indian Subcontinent and South East Asia where the British established a colonial administration and its attendant education system (English medium), an educated (in the 'Western' sense) group became accustomed to using English as their medium of communication: among their own peer group and for national and international communication. As a local media grew, and a literature in English, so the importance of the form grew.

These NNFs are distinctive – they have their own internal grammatical coherence, pronunciation system, lexis and discourse features. Examples of discourse features would include the way in which an argument is presented or a topic in conversation is changed, etc. Prescriptivists would argue that these NNFs are corruptions of the 'mother' standard variety of English. Pluralists, on the other hand, would argue that these NNFs do not prevent their users from engaging in a rich inner-life and cultural discourse with their countrymen and the world at large. (See Wells, 1982; Platt, Weber and Ho, 1984; Todd and Hancock, 1986; and Trudgill and Hannah, 1993, for detailed descriptions of NNFs.)

TASKS

A)   Collect as many examples as you can of 'incorrect English'. Make a note of their origins, and where you came across them. Check on their acceptability with native speakers and non-native speakers. Also, check their grammaticality with relevant reference books.

B) Collect new words and expressions that you come across in English, especially in non-native forms (NNFs). Classify them according to their origin, the commonality of their use and their acceptability for native and non-native speakers alike.

Thinking questions
1) What are your feelings with regard to the reactions of other language users to questions of acceptability and grammaticality? Do you find your own views modified or strengthened by others' views on these subjects?
2) What do you think is the basis for people's views on grammaticality and acceptability? Try to list as many points as you can.

C) Choose an area of the world previously colonized by Britain. Research the variety of English spoken there in terms of its form, lexicon and social uses. Check English dictionaries for vernacular words which have entered the English lexicon from your chosen study area.
What do your researches tell you about language development and change?

Learning English

Aim To examine our attitudes and ideas about learning English and other languages.

The previous sections have explored language from the points of view of its users, particularly yourself and, in a lesser sense, from the analyst's point of view. A key point to emerge from these activities is that our knowledge and attitudes as users of language strongly influence our analytical faculties, in particular our notions of correctness and acceptability and appropriateness.

This section introduces professional issues in language teaching and learning. This set of activities examines various views about learning a foreign language (namely, English), drawing on ideas from linguistic description and teaching methodology.

ACTIVITY 1.13

Examine the following statements. They have all been made at one time or another by teachers and learners of English.

1) English is a very irregular language. It is therefore difficult for a non-native speaker to learn.

2) When a native speaker and a non-native speaker of English converse in English, this is an authentic use of the language by both parties.

3) The British seem very tolerant of non-natives' use of English. It is thus difficult for the non-native speaker to get feedback on whether or not they are using English correctly when speaking to an English person.

4) If a person does not know English, it will be difficult for that person to participate in today's world.

5) Without a knowledge of grammar, it is difficult to see a student progressing in their learning of a language.

6) Memorizing lists of words is not a particularly helpful learning strategy for the non-native speaker.

Thinking questions
Do you see a consistent pattern in your responses to the statements? Are you a 'purist' (keen to preserve standards) or a 'pluralist' (content to see many different varieties of English coexist)?

ACTIVITY 1.14

Which of the attitudes about teaching and learning grammar and vocabulary as expressed below is: (1) most similar to your own; (2) most different from yours; (3) most common in your community (local or national).

Grammar
1) It's a waste of time teaching grammar – it only confuses the students and uses up valuable class time which we could be using for the teaching of skills.

2) Without grammar, there is no language learning. It is the backbone of the whole process.

3) Although we need to be aware of the importance of grammar, we should not teach it directly. It is best learned by indirect exposure to the target language.

4) Grammar is the only part of a language which we can be sure about; to ignore it is a sort of madness.

5) If we are teaching students to communicate, grammar is of no real use.

Vocabulary
1) Most vocabulary is picked up during encounters with native speakers of a language, or by reading books by native speakers.

2) It is impossible to demonstrate the meaning of items in L2 vocabulary without a context.

3) There are many items of vocabulary in any given language which cannot be

translated into another language. Thus when we are learning vocabulary, we are also learning cultural and social knowledge.

4) The use and possession of a wide vocabulary in a language is a mark of a high degree of proficiency in the language (by a native or non-native speaker).

5) Speakers of all languages (native or non-native) have strategies for compensating for the lack of vocabulary.

Thinking questions

1) Can you identify different types of attitude in the sets above? For example, are some *social* attitudes? Are there any which might be termed '*psychological*'? Are there also any which comment on the individual and their language learning abilities or potential?

2) What sorts of attitude are a deterrent to people learning foreign languages? Are there any expressed in the statements above?

3) How might teachers and learners seek to overcome negative attitudes towards learning among their students of foreign languages?

4) What sorts of attitude do you think might have positive effects on language learning (individual, intellectual or social)?

Further ideas

For many years, the business of language teaching has blended the findings of two major disciplines for its underlying rationale. Descriptive linguistics has tended to provide the categories for the *content* of language teaching, for example, 'structures' and 'functions', and psychology has either directly or indirectly provided the rationale for different ways and means of teaching and learning – *methods* – for example, 'direct method'. In practice, therefore, a certain description of, say, 'structures' of English has been married to a behavioural view of psychology with its emphasis on habit formation through repeated practice of those structures in the target language.

Recent shifts of opinion have challenged these views:

1) Our views of language – what it is and how it works. The focus has broadened from a concentration on descriptions which work only at sentence level to a large collection of techniques for trying to understand discourse, or language use above the level of sentence. The professional linguist, as well as asking basic descriptive questions, is now asking questions derived from an interpretive view of language in context (speakers both comprehend and interpret the language user's meaning and intention when it is used in context), seeking an understanding of why speakers use language in the ways they do. This interest in understanding language use applies equally to the forms of the language as it does to its sociocultural meanings.

2) We have also become more interested in *how* learners learn. The behaviourist's view that learning was a matter of stimulus and response does

not account for the cognitive and affective domains of learning. Where previously in language learning the focus was on 'effective teaching', and how this could best be achieved with groups of learners using specific standardized methods, the emphasis is now on learners, as individuals first and foremost. Questions as to how learners process language and how they manage their learning in social settings are centre stage. Thus language teaching professionals are concerned with exploring methodology, or how to create the most productive conditions for language learning inside and outside the classroom.

These shifts of focus, outlined above, have given rise to some degree of uncertainty in language teaching circles as to which descriptions of language and which ideas about learning are most useful, rewarding and generative. In these circumstances, and also to explore the notion of methodology deeply, there seems to be, more than ever, a need for knowledge which can assist in coping with the uncertainty. The more open-ended and plural our descriptions of language and learning, the more protagonists in language teaching and learning encounters need to know about language learning, and the more subtle and probing need to be their analyses of language. In addition, teachers' responses to learners' needs as learners place increasing strains upon teachers' resources. Teachers may need to be, more than ever, resourceful, sympathetic and willing to learn themselves. One way in which they can achieve this is through an increasing awareness of language, and how it operates and is used.

TASKS

1)   Work with an informant (non-native speaker of a language — preferably English) and try to find out what sorts of view or attitude they draw on when learning a foreign language. Use the statements above to help you produce questions. In addition, create your own questions on the basis of your reflections on the second language/foreign language learning process.

2)   Examine the extracts which follow and note the views of the authors on the nature of language and the nature of learning. Which do you find most sympathy with?

   A. The learner does not embark upon his second language learning experience as a *tabula rasa* or in total ignorance of everything concerning language and what we use it for. What he does bring to this initial language-learning task is a kind of prior knowledge of two different sorts. One sort we might describe as 'knowledge that' — an unconscious 'foreknowledge' or innate 'inkling' of what shapes the organisation of the target language can assume — and the capacity, given a little start in the new language, to make good guesses about what he *doesn't* know (Rutherford, 1987:7–8).

B. A second language learner's knowledge of a second language forms a systematic whole (Spolksy, 1989:31).

C. Second language learner language approximates native speaker language (Spolsky, 1989:35).

D. When a student is exposed to a new language, the first internal hurdles are posed by the individual's emotional state and motivations (Dulay, Burt and Krashen, 1982:4).

E. While learners are engaged in an effort to understand and express meaning, a process of internal system-development is hypothesized to go on at a sub-conscious level of their minds (Prabhu, 1987:69).

Thinking question

What can we learn about language and language learning from looking at the efforts of second language learners? (For example, what can we learn about grammar, vocabulary or discourse and how it is learned?) Work with a language learner and try to establish how they learn and cope with learning. Wenden and Rubin (1987) contains several useful ideas on how to do this.

Activity 1.9 – Key

Examples 1–4 } Such utterances are found in the speech of
6–11 } many English native speakers, particularly in
15–23 } London and the south-east of England. Many of these are also 'carried' to written English where they may be judged less acceptable. 16 is both grammatical and acceptable.

Examples 5, 13, 14   These utterances are widely accepted in the Indian variety of English.

Example 12   'drinkability' is typical of the words invented by the advertising industry.

Activity 1.12 – Key

movious (Zambian/Malawian English)	– very mobile; moves around a lot from place to place [can have negative connotations]
a go-down (Malaysian English)	– large warehouse
on seat (West African English)	– present [usually at work]
a bottlestore (South African English)	– small shop selling mainly alcoholic drinks
a bioscope (South African English)	– cinema
download ("computerese")	– transfer information from a central computer memory to portable disks
plannification (Many NNFs)	– planning
regionalization (British/American English)	– diffusion of power away from the capital of a country to regions
a mealie (Central and South African English)	– maize cob
to fair out (Indian English)	– write a fair copy
walkative (Zambian English)	– travels long distances on foot

2

Systems, structures and meanings in English

Introduction

This chapter aims to engage you in an exploration of various aspects of English grammar and structure. The activities call upon your existing knowledge and understanding of English grammar, and assist you in refining and developing your knowledge and understanding. Above all, I hope your sensitivity to various aspects of English (in general) is enhanced, as well as your awareness of how specific points work. This chapter does not attempt to cover every aspect or corner of what is traditionally called 'English grammar'. Rather, we shall explore various ways of analysing and examining language with a limited range of topics. It is hoped that the skills and awareness that develop from these explorations will help you to approach any area of English in future.

In addition to engaging your views about English grammar, we shall also encounter the views of grammarians, language teachers and linguists. As wide a range of views as possible has been provided, in order to assist you in making up your own mind about the issues in question. As well as information, these views are designed to provide material to analyse and evaluate.

In addition to active 'doing' and analytical activities, there are also both reflective and thinking activities. At these points you are invited to pause and use the questions provided to help you put into perspective various ideas about language and the activities you have done. This is an opportunity to make sense of the activities and to move tentatively towards conclusions about the points under investigation.

Finally, further ideas on many of the topics are offered. These are provided to enable you to extend and consolidate your knowledge in these areas. They offer both 'technical' and 'personal' insights into the areas under consideration. They are not a commentary to the activities as such, and may even present counter-arguments to some of the conclusions you have reached while doing the exercises.

Note While you may normally wish to work through a topic in the sequence of activities as suggested by the number system, you may also want to devise your own routes through the exercises. You can, for example, begin with the 'Further ideas' sections and then move to the exploration of data. A further alternative is to begin with the 'Thinking questions' before moving on to the data analysis and exploration.

Getting the language right

Aim   To examine grammatical terminology used in reference grammars, which will be helpful for you to use in your own work with language as learner, teacher or both.

ACTIVITY 2.1

1)   Match the items in the left-hand column with the items in the right-hand column in order to create a matrix of terms to describe language and its components, patterns and systems. An example is done for you.

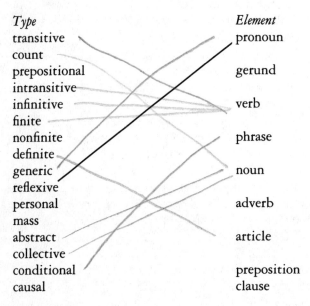

Type	*Element*
transitive	pronoun
count	
prepositional	gerund
intransitive	
infinitive	verb
finite	
nonfinite	phrase
definite	
generic	noun
reflexive	
personal	adverb
mass	
abstract	article
collective	
conditional	preposition
causal	clause

2)   Give one or two examples of each of the combinations you have found, or know about (e.g., reflexive pronoun – 'himself'). Note any of the elements in the right-hand column which cannot be qualified in any way with an item from the 'type' column. What is the significance of these 'isolated elements'? Does it, for instance, mean that there is only one type of this element? Or does it mean that we need other 'type' terms to describe it?

Are there any terms which you know but which have not appeared in the exercise above? Note these.

Thinking questions

1) What is the value of the matrix of grammatical terminology? To you personally? To a student of English? To a teacher of English?
2) Are there any problems or dangers associated with grammatical terminology that you are aware of? For the teacher? For the student?
3) How do you react when you find the same linguistic phenomena described in different ways in different reference grammars? Choose an item (e.g., 'reflexive pronouns') and look it up in different reference grammars.

Further ideas

Grammatical descriptions are changing

Many descriptions of English employ a 'Latinate' set of terminology. This is not so surprising in view of the fact that early attempts to write grammars of English were steeped in the Latin descriptive system. Not only are these descriptions often inaccurate (trying to squeeze a hybrid language like English with its origins in Anglo-Saxon, with strong traces of Greek, Latin and other European languages into a Latinate description has disadvantages: the hybrid language has many inconsistencies which do not match the apparent regularity of Latin), but they are also misleading. Grammatical categories such as *gender, case* and *mood* (for example) work differently in Latin compared with English. There are also scholars who seek to describe the subjunctive and dative case in English. Again these work differently in English. In recent years, however, there has been a move among grammarians to develop categories which attempt to describe and account for aspects of English function and use, rather than formal categories.

Many contemporary descriptions of English are based firmly on corpus studies – that is, studies of examples drawn from instances of 'real' language use in society, particularly written forms. (You might consider why it is more difficult to work with a spoken corpus.) As a consequence, new grammatical and other categories are beginning to emerge, depending on the stance adopted by the grammarians. For example, a 'lexical' view of English has yielded the Grammar of Contemporary English (GCE, 1972) and more recently the 'Cobuild' grammar (1990), with new categories such as 'noun modifiers' (e.g., *'car* door'), which describe how certain elements of the grammatical system behave in real language use. A 'communicative' or semantic view of English has established categories such as 'manner, means and instrument' (Leech and Svartvik (1975)). What both these new approaches share in common is a focus on *meaning.* Traditional grammar focused largely on form, aided by the notion that even form was regular and open to categorization in terms drawn from grammars of other apparently more regular languages.

TASKS

Jargon-spotting

Go through (1) the contents page and (2) a sample unit or chapter of a typical English (or other language) coursebook in use in your educational context and list the grammatical terminology used. Make sure you are familiar with the meanings of the various terminology by checking in reference grammars. Use the example contents page which follows for a trial run.

Contents

Introduction

Verbs
  1 Present continuous
  2 Present simple
  3 Present continuous and present simple
  4 Past simple
  5 Past continuous
  6 Present perfect simple
  7 *Gone* and *been*
  8 Present perfect with *just, yet* and *already*
  9 Present perfect continuous
  10 Present perfect continuous and present perfect simple
  11 Present perfect with *for* and *since*
  12 Present perfect and past simple
  13 Present perfect and present tense
  14 Past perfect simple
  15 Past perfect continuous
  16 Future: *will*
  17 Future: *going to*
  18 Future: *will* and *going to*
  19 Present continuous for the future
  20 Future: present continuous and *going to*

  38 Obligation and necessity (1): *must, have to, have got to*
  39 Obligation and necessity (2): *mustn't, don't have to, don't need to, haven't got to, needn't*
  40 Review of permission and obligation: *can, can't, must, mustn't, needn't, be allowed to, have to, don't have to*
  41 *Needn't have* and *didn't need to*
  42 Obligation and advice: *should, ought to, had better, be supposed to, shall*
  43 Possibility: *may, might, could*
  44 Possibility: *can*

45 Probability: *should, ought to*
46 Deduction: *must, can't*
47 Review of possibility, probability and deduction: *may, might, could, should, ought to, must, can't*
48 Requests: *can, could, may, will, would*
49 Offers: *will, shall, can, could, would*
50 Suggestions: *shall, let's, why don't we? how/what about? can, could*
51 Habits: *used to, will, would*
52 Refusals: *won't, wouldn't*
53 Promises and threats: *will*

(Beaumont and Granger, 1989)

How words work

Aim   To examine the different grammatical properties words can have and to establish some of the main directions and concepts in the study of language systems and their uses.

ACTIVITY 2.2

Word classes

1)   What word classes (noun, verb, preposition, etc.) do each of the words in the list below fall into? More than one class is possible for each item.

> watch   me   laughing   attack   bounce   goal   himself   go   slick
> chart   red   however   sun   in   onto   well   bigger   smart   one
> upwards   will   tiger   a   every   must

2)   Comment on the grammatical properties of each of the words above. You might like to consider the following, for example:

- Whether the word automatically precedes or follows another, in a set sequence (e.g., 'on' is often followed by a noun in a phrase like 'on edge' or preceded by a verb, as in 'pick on').
- Whether the word could conceivably stand alone and make sense used in that way (e.g., 'Fire!' when uttered as a warning).
- Whether adding an element to the word like '-*ing*' at the end of a word is possible, and if this changes the grammatical meaning of the word (e.g. He is *walking* or *walking* is good for you).

- Whether there are certain word classes that an item cannot keep close company with (e.g., a preposition cannot form a grammatical phrase with only an adverb as in '*in luckily').

ACTIVITY 2.3

Can you divide the words in the list in Activity 2.2 into two broad groups, according to their basic grammatical properties as words? What are the main properties of the words in each of your two groups?

Thinking questions
1) What should an informed user of a language know about the grammatical properties of words? Use insights gained from Activities 2.2 and 2.3 to formulate a response. How valuable are the categories?
2) Can individual words have more than one meaning, as well as operating in more than one grammatical class?
3) Is a description of English based on words alone likely to be sufficient?

Further ideas

Different types of grammatical rule
Grammatical rules specify a number of features and operations. It may help if we distinguish between some basic types of grammatical rule. (We should not by the way be surprised or perturbed if we notice a few exceptions to these rules – some of these will be exemplified in the section which follows.) For our purposes here, 'grammatical' includes any specification of syntax (such as word order) as well as rules which refer to different word classes (such as agreement).

Example 1 Word order
In English there are rules of word order. For example:

Adj + Noun
big   foot

although

Noun + Adj
something   hot (in '*I'd like something hot.*')

Pronoun + Auxiliary + Verb
I   am   singing

Example 2 Agreement
In English the main agreement rules specify. For example:

singular and plural (nouns & verbs)

he eat*s* well

they eat well (although 'Three years *is* a long time')

auxiliary tense and main verb (agreement between pronoun and auxiliary rather than verb). For example:

he *is* eating

he *has* eaten

There may be difficulties for users of English in understanding or creating complex sentences which contain more than one propositon, when rules of word order, negation, agreement, clause structure, etc. meet. The user is faced with not one, but many rules to decode in one relatively restricted context. For example: 'Without realising the potential consequences of going ahead with the plan, the men, who were tired and cold, leapt into the fray'.

This example is, in actuality, several propositions linked by grammatical devices into a unit of meaning. Try writing a separate sentence for each of the different propositions contained in it.

Word classes

In English, words can appear in different word classes. For example, a noun like 'dog' can be used as a verb with an idiomatic meaning – 'He was dogged by ill luck'. The word 'well' can operate as a noun, a verb and an adverb –

'A well was drilled in our village.'

'Tears welled up in her eyes.'

'He's well placed to take over the captaincy.'

(In recent years, 'well' has also become a modifier – 'He's well strong' – in the London Variety.)

Polysemic items (or items with many meanings) further complicate the picture. The item 'pick' operates as a noun and a verb, and has multiple meanings in both word classes.

New words 1 (see also Further ideas in 1.6)

New words can emerge in several ways:

1) Completely new item (e.g. xerox) [new objects or activities]
2) Extension of word class (e.g. lift) [both noun and verb]
3) Word creation (e.g. deplane)
4) Change in word meaning (e.g. fire)

New words in the CLOSED classes of English (i.e. the grammatical – auxiliaries, articles etc.) are very uncommon and emerge only very slowly as a rule (although 'Ms.' has entered the system of address forms extremely quickly). For example, 'you' has replaced 'thou' (common in the 19th century). New items occur more readily in the lexicon – nouns, main verbs (lexical verbs), adjectives, adverbs – the OPEN classes.

English words may be classified as in Figure 2.1. There is a core of grammatical items which 'bind' the lexical items together. Information and meaning is transmitted by both sets – about, for example, time in the verb group, and about direction by some prepositions.

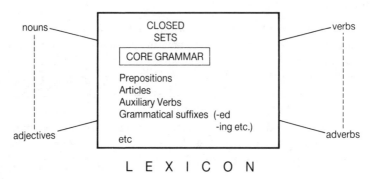

FIG. 2.1   The organization of English words.

ACTIVITY 2.4

Pieces of words
Look at the following list of words. Try to divide each word into parts, according to the following criteria:

1) Different elements of *meaning*.
2) Different 'chunks' of sound when the word is spoken.
3) Any other significant elements you notice.

> unsatisfactorily   laptop   proclaimer   advantageous   unyielding
> extremely   surfer   geological   eulogize   wasted   grammarian
> timetable   written   asymmetrical   unbecoming   personified

---

Thinking questions
1) In what ways can the insights you have reached in this activity be of help to speakers (native and non-native), learners and teachers of English respectively?
2) Are there ways in which the speakers of a language use the 'rules' of word formation creatively?

3) Are there sometimes ways in which speakers can misuse the rules of word formation?

Further ideas

Prefixes, etc.
These small elements of words carry both/either grammatical or semantic information. They bind like molecules to the core of items (Figure 2.2). Check the list in Activity 2.4 to see if it conforms to these 'rules'.

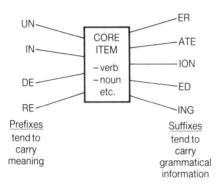

FIG. 2.2 Prefixes and suffixes.

New words 2
Many new words are formed by creative use of the prefixes, etc. (see 'deplanc' in 'New words 1', above). Also there are new items which combine two nouns ('pickaxe' or an adjective + noun – 'coldstore'). Both these tendencies are at work in contemporary English. Check, in particular, texts on 'modern' activities such as computing or surfing. A new vocabulary emerges, using the basic grammar of English, but exploiting word formation rules to transmit new messages. For example:

software
wordprocessing
toolkit
workstation
cursor
spreadsheet
motherboard
access
read/write head
standalone

Check any computing magazine/publication for further 'new words'. (Collect new words from the media, or specialist texts.)

TASK

Analyse the short text which follows in the following ways:

1) Eliminate all 'grammatical words' or parts of words. What is the effect on the text? Can you still understand the text? Are there some parts of the text which become more difficult to understand than others?
2) Describe the grammatical word class of every word in the first part of the text in as much detail as you are able. Do you feel a need to group items in sets in order to account for how they are used?
3) Can you identify any words in the text which have been 'built' using the rules of word formation?
4) Are there any 'new' words or phrases in English (words with a contemporary or recent origin)?

Which School for your Child?

Parents! Are you looking for a school for your children? Among the wide choice available have you considered the independent schools?

5   You may find that there is one which would especially suit your individual child.

There has been a notable growth of interest in these schools over the past 10 year or two. They are purposeful and well disciplined. Classes are small so that each child can be treated as an individual. They provide a very wide range of extra-curricular oppor-15 tunities. Contact with parents is close, because they stand or fall by providing what the parents pay for.

Parents who are familiar with independent schools in general may need 20 help to find the particular one they need. Others may find general guidance helpful.

An ideal source of sensitive advice is ISIS: the Independent Schools Infor-25 mation Services [. . .].

They will tell you where the schools are, what they are like, what they cost and what may be the advantages. There are boys', girls' and co-30 educational schools; senior and junior schools and schools for children of all ages from seven to 18 (*Plympton, Plymstock and Ivybridge News*, 20 November 1992).

Thinking questions

1) What have you learned from these activities about the way in which English words are 'built' or structured?
2) What value do you see in analysing English according to a system of word classes and structures? For whom might this analysis be of value?

A matter of time

Aim   To examine the relationships between the ways in which our concepts of time are expressed through the verb system and other means in English.

ACTIVITY 2.5

1)   Identify the *verbs* in the short text which follows. It is the text of an announcement heard at a railway station in Britain.

> THE INTERCITY SERVICE FOR BRISTOL CALLING AT PLATFORM FOUR IS RUNNING 17 – 17 – MINUTES LATE. WE APOLOGIZE TO PASSENGERS FOR ANY INCONVENIENCE THIS WILL HAVE CAUSED.

2)   Account for the *forms* and *meanings* of the *verbs* in the announcement. Pay particular attention to the time reference of each verb: is the announcement referring to past, present or future time? Think about this question from the points of view of both speaker and listener.

3)   Identify any other part of the text which has either a direct or indirect reference to time. How do these other time references relate to the verbs in the text? Do they qualify or modify the time references of the verbs?

4)   Try changing the tenses of the verbs in the text in various ways. What is the effect of any changes that you make?

Thinking questions

What is 'difficult' about the verb system in English compared with the verb system in any other language you know? Why is it, do you think, that the English verb system causes so many difficulties for so many people who learn English as a second language?

ACTIVITY 2.6

1)   Read through the extracts from selected reference grammars of English below. Using the information you find there, draw up working definitions of the following terms: *time, tense, aspect.* Write these out and compare them with those of colleagues. Give one or two illustrations from the English verb system of each term. As you work through the section *Verbs and time,* you may find these definitions useful. If you do go from this section to *Verbs and time,* you may wish to refine the definitions as you do the activities in the latter section.

A. **Time, tense and aspect**

103

We turn now to features of tense and aspect expressed by the verb phrase. Tense and aspect ... relate the happening described by the verb to time in the past, present, or future.

States and events
104

Since tense relates the meaning of the verb to a time scale, we must first give some attention to the different kinds of meaning a verb may have. Broadly, verbs may refer either to an EVENT (*ie* a happening thought of as a single occurrence, with a definite beginning and end), or to a STATE (*ie* a state of affairs which continues over a period, and need not have a well-defined beginning and end).

Thus *be, live, stay, know, etc* may be considered STATE VERBS, and *get, come, leave, hit, etc* EVENT VERBS. This distinction is similar to the distinction between count and mass nouns, and (as we saw in ... for count and mass), it is to some extent a conceptual rather than a real distinction. The same verb can change from one category to another, and the distinction is not always clear: *Did you remember his name?* could refer either to a state or to an event.

To be more accurate, then, we should talk of 'state uses of verbs' and 'event uses of verbs'; but it is convenient to keep to the simpler terms 'state verb' and 'event verb'.

105

The distinction between 'state' and 'event' gives rise to the following three basic kinds of verb meaning (illustrated in the past tense):

(1)	STATE	Napoleon was a Corsican
(2)	SINGLE EVENT	Columbus discovered America
(3)	SET OF REPEATED EVENTS (HABIT)	Paganini played the violin

The 'habit' meaning combines 'event' meaning with 'state' meaning: a habit is, in a sense, a state consisting of a series of events. We often specify 'state' meaning by adding an adverbial of duration: *Queen Victoria reigned for sixty-four years.* We specify 'habit' more precisely by adding an adverbial of frequency or an adverbial of duration: *He played the violin every day from the age of five.* (All three types of meaning can be clarified by an adverbial of time-when, see ...)

To these three a further type of verbal meaning can be added, the TEMPORARY meaning expressed by the progressive aspect (see ...): *She was cooking the dinner* (Leech and Svartvick, 1975: 64–65).

B. **5.1**   When you are making a statement, you usually need to indicate whether you are referring to a situation which exists now, existed in the past, or is likely to exist in the future. The point in time that a statement relates to is usually indicated in part by the **verb group** used in the clause.

A set of verb forms that indicate a particular point in time or period of time in the past, present, or future is called a **tense**.

The set of forms belonging to a particular tense is usually obtained by the addition of **inflections** to the base form of the verb, or by the inclusion of **auxiliaries** or **modals** in the verb group.

smile ... smiled
was smiling ... has been smiling ... had smiled
will smile ... may smile

Some verbs have irregular forms for past tenses.

fight ... fighting ... fought
go ... going ... went

(*Collins Cobuild English Grammar*, 1990: 245)

2)   Make a list of all the ways in English in which *time* is referred to, both directly and indirectly. Use your reference grammar if you need to.

3)(a)   (*If English is not your mother tongue*)   What are the main differences between the verb system in your native language (L1) and English? (You may want to think about *form* (or *structure*) as well as the *use* and *meaning* of each form in your native tongue.)

(b)   (*If you are a native speaker of English*)   Refer throughout this part of the activity to a second or foreign language with which you are familiar. What are the main differences between the verb system in the foreign language and English. (You may want to think about *form* (or *structure*) as well as the *use* and *meaning* of each form in your native tongue.)

Think about your L1 3(a) or the foreign language 3(b) *as if describing it to a non-native speaker of that language.*

Thinking questions
1)   Do you think that grammatical differences between languages, or conceptual problems with the ways in which time is expressed by verbs, are serious problems for learners of second languages?
2)   Can you express your ideas about time without being strictly correct grammatically with respect to verb tense usage?

Further ideas

. . . most people would agree that in the English language, the most troublesome problems are concentrated in the area of the finite verb phrase, and include, in particular, questions of tense, aspect and modal auxiliary usage (Leech, 1971:v).

. . . almost all English verb forms are generated by a combination of a small number of structural features, each of which has clearly defined and identifiable primary semantic characteristics (Lewis, 1986:163).

The verb is the pivot in English?

More has been written about the English verb than any other component of the language. This may be explained by

- its apparent structural complexity;
- its link with meaning, conveyed through tense and aspect; and
- the difficulty posed by verbs for people trying to learn English.

Not only do verbs describe actions and states or conditions in reality but also the grammatical elements (e.g., '-*ed*' endings in the regular simple past tense) give further information about time. The verb may be characterized as the pivotal point in any utterance, around which other grammatical components revolve. The verb, for example, helps to establish the nature of relationships between people, objects and entities in the real world. For example:

John — a driver.
is . . . (*linking*) (*state*) John is the driver.
called . . . (*dynamic*) (*event*) John is not the driver.

Without the verb, we cannot arrive at an accurate interpretation of '*John a driver'. Remove all trace of verbs from a text and it begins to appear like a strange shopping list (unless we are familiar with the context, however). Remove all the nouns or pronouns and the grammatical elements of verbs and we are left with a series of unattributed actions and states, both in time and personally. The language of advertising slogans e.g. 'Better Buy Bold'; 'Drives the Imagination Wild' either seems to reduce verbs to the simple present form or leaves their grammatical class vague – is 'buy' a noun or a verb, or both?

Perceptions of time

Do people from different cultural backgrounds perceive time differently? Or do they have differing attitudes towards time? Or both? If there are differences, do they manifest themselves in the verb systems of different languages? It is unlikely that people perceive clear boundaries between past, present and future. These are reference points in every English speaker's vocabulary which also happen to be part of grammatical description. Whether there is a total coincidence between them is another matter altogether.

Time is all-enveloping; events are transitory. As I write this, and as you read it, it becomes part of our collective and shared past. But it was my past before it was yours. It had a future potential. As you read it in your present time, it becomes past. Because it is stored in print form, however, it retains its future potential. Both you and I can come back to it at any time unspecified in the future. The event is transitory, but the knowledge is now preserved. Speakers and writers always have a temporal stance: speakers always speak in the present, and many events are seen from this standpoint. Speakers are also able to project themselves into the past or future and see things 'as if'. [This will be further explored in *Verbs and time*].

It is possible that in an agricultural society, time has different meanings and interpretations than in industrial society. Both such cultures exist in the British Isles, and both use English to express their experience of that reality. They may accord different meanings to the verb forms because of different cultural patterns. How much should we read into the fact that Arabic has only 'complete' and 'incomplete' verb forms? Does this mean that Arabic speakers do not understand the past? Highly dubious!

The second language learner is, however, faced with a new network of forms and meanings in the verb system in the new language, which is different from the mother tongue. The experience can transform the commonplace to the exotic.

ACTIVITY 2.7

1) Study the samples, taken from widely used reference grammars of English, and comment on how each one provides information about the verb system, noting terminology used and the way in which the information is presented in each case.

Note similarities and differences between the ways in which the different grammars deal with the point of reference in the samples.
2) Which presentation do you prefer? What criteria informed your choice? (*Optional* Prepare a simple advertisement for your preferred reference grammar – consult the grammar if you are not already familiar with it – to appeal to non-native speaker learners of English at a level of your choice.)

A. **Tense, aspect and mood**
3.26

Time is a universal, non-linguistic concept with three divisions: past, present and future; by *tense* we understand the correspondence between the form of the verb and our concept of time. *Aspect* concerns the manner in which the verbal action is experienced or regarded (for example as completed or in progress), while *mood* relates the verbal action to such conditions as certainty, obligation, necessity, possibility. In fact, however, to a great extent these three categories impinge on each other: in particular, the expression of time present and past cannot be considered separately from aspect, and the expression of the future is closely bound up with mood.

Tense and aspect
3.27
We here consider the *present* and *past* tenses in relation to the *progressive* and *perfective* aspects. The range can be seen in the sentence frame 'I — with a special pen', filling the blank with a phrase having the verb base *write*:

	SIMPLE	COMPLEX	
		progressive	
present	write	am writing	*present*
		was writing	*past*
		perfective	
		have written	*(present) perfect*
past	wrote	had written	*past (or plu-) perfect*
		perfect progressive	
		have been writing	*(present) perfect*
		had been writing	*past (or plu-) perfect*

(Quirk and Greenbaum (1973: 40/41)

B. 9 Verbs, verb tenses, imperatives

General information about verbs and tenses

9.1 What a verb is and what it does
A verb is a word (*run*) or a phrase (*run out of*) which expresses the existence of a state (*love, seem*) or the doing of an action (*take, play*). Two facts are basic:
1 Verbs are used to express distinctions in time (past, present, future) through **tense** (often with adverbials of time or frequency).
2 Auxiliary verbs … are used with full verbs to give other information about actions and states. For example *be* may be used with the present participle of a full verb to say that an action was going on ('in progress') at a particular time (*I was swimming*); *have* may be used with the past participle of a full verb to say that an action is completed (*I have finished*).

9.2 Verb tenses: simple and progressive
Some grammarians believe that tense must always be shown by the actual form of the verb, and in many languages present, past and future are indicated by changes in the verb forms. On this reckoning, English really has just two tenses, the present and the past, since these are the only two cases where the form of the basic verb varies: *love, write* (present); *loved, wrote* (past).
However, it is usual (and convenient) to refer to all combinations of *be* + present participle and *have* + past participle as tenses. The same goes for

will + bare infinitive ... to refer to the future (*It will be fine tomorrow*). But we must remember that tense in English is often only loosely related to time.

Tenses have two forms, **simple** and **progressive** (sometimes called 'continuous'). The progressive contains *be* + present participle:

	simple	**progressive**	
present:	*I work.*	*I am*	*working.*
past:	*I worked.*	*I was*	*working.*
present perfect:	*I have worked.*	*I have been*	*working.*
past perfect:	*I had worked.*	*I had been*	*working.*
future:	*I will work.*	*I will be*	*working.*
future perfect:	*I will have worked.*	*I will have been*	*working.*

(Alexander, 1988: 159)

Thinking questions
1) In what ways can a reference grammar help you analyse linguistic problems? Give some examples.
2) Why do you think there are differences of approach between reference grammars? Look at a selection of reference grammars in order to verify your ideas.

Further ideas

Reference grammars
Reference grammars provide descriptions of language for scholars, students and interested lay users. They tend, however, to differ, both in form and in content. The main points of difference are as follows:

1) Different terminology is used to describe the same phenomena.
2) Different explanations are given for the same phenomena.
3) Different grammars operate at different levels of complexity.
4) Some grammars cover more points than others. Rarely is a grammar all-embracing, and only rarely does it claim to be (see *Comprehensive Grammar of English*). Levels of coverage and detail vary considerably.
5) The contents are arranged in a different order in every grammar.

These points might seem insignificant, but for the user they can be very important. Compilers of reference grammars are putting forward their particular points of view about grammar and language – they cannot all be wrong or all be right. The user may be left in doubt by an entry; the description may not coincide with a previous idea the user had; an entry may not entirely match with the facts of an instance of use; and so on. Grammars also attempt to move with the times. 'Communicative' grammars are a recent phenomenon, coinciding with the spate of descriptions of language as communication – but the terminology might be alien to the user, used to a more 'traditional' description.

TASKS

1)   Choose a reference grammar of English from the list given in the 'Further reading' section. Write a short review of the work for a student who is looking for a grammar to accompany their studies of English.

Begin by stating some criteria for evaluating the grammar. Then match the grammar against the criteria. Choose one or two examples from the sections which deal with verbs to accompany your view. [Refer to Chalker (1984) for further ideas]

2)   Collect advertising slogans – from the radio, television, magazines etc. Examine the use of verbs in the slogans – for example, what is the predominant tense used? Are there verbless slogans?

Verbs and time

Aim   To examine the relationships between verbs and time in English.

ACTIVITY 2.8

Using, teaching and learning English verbs
Aim   To elicit readers' attitudes and beliefs about various aspects of the verb system in English.

What is your opinion about each of the statements (heard and overheard) which follow? Do you agree or disagree? Wholly? Partly? Note your reasoning in each case.

1)   The present simple tells us that an action is habitual. The present continuous tells us that an action is happening right *now*.
2)   The present tense is the easiest to understand and teach. This is because it is the most commonly used.
3)   The main difficulty with the way in which English deals with present time is the way it differentiates in the verb system between permanent conditions and temporary incidents.

4) Teaching and learning the past tense in English is a pretty straightforward matter.
5) My students don't know whether the past perfect is a structural or a conceptual device in English.
6) The present perfect is so difficult that most of my students give up trying to learn it. Why can't we just use the past tense?
7) There is no future tense in English. That's the big problem for second language speakers.
8) The English are very exact when they talk about the future. That's because they are very organized people.

Thinking questions
1) With reference to the eight statements in Activity 2.8 and your responses to them, make a list of the main problem areas in the English verb system from the point of view of teaching and learning English as a second or foreign language.
2) Do you see the English verb system as a system of *concepts* or as a system of linguistic *forms*? Or is it a combination?
3) Are you at ease with the idea that *meaning* is a central focus of the study of English verbs? Can you explain your response?

ACTIVITY 2.9

Aim This activity focuses on various elements of the English verb system through an examination of types of error.

Examine the sentences which follow. They all contain possible errors in the verb group, which is in italic in each case.

A) Identify the errors and say whether they are errors of *structure* (or *form*) or of *use*.

Can you offer explanations for the errors? Keep a careful record of the terms you have used to describe the errors. Use a table like the one below the examples to record your answers.

B) Identify sentences which could be acceptable, depending on the context in which they appear. Explain how they might be acceptable.

1) *She *looking* for her spectacles.
2) *I *am thinking* you are wrong.
3) *Do *you eating* meat?
4) *At the moment *they build* a new teaching block.
5) *I *am having* three brothers.
6) *I *not liking* tea with milk.
7) *I *am play* football very well.

8) *He speak* English very well.
9) *I didn't fell.*
10) *The children *had played* noisily.
11) *I *have travelled* to work by train.
12) *Alfred *mended* his fence when I saw him.
13) *Jules *was knowing* the answer but told nobody.
14) *The bus *was arriving.*
15) *I *will be go.*
16) *I *going* to go.
17)   A: When are you going home?
    *B: *I will go* home tomorrow.
18)   A: When does your plane leave?
    *B: *It's going to* leave at six in the evening.
19) *Annie *will have married* for six years tomorrow.

Example	Form or use	Correct version	Description of error

Thinking questions

1) If you are a teacher of English as a second or foreign language, do your students make errors like those above? Identify specific items. Do they tend to be errors of form or use? Do you think speakers of English as their mother tongue make errors like these?

2) Do you think it is of value to a teacher and a student to be able to describe and explain errors? Are there any potential barriers between teachers and students which might impede understanding of errors? What do errors tell us (about language and about learning)?

Further ideas

Verb meaning

In addition to the grammatical identification of different aspects of time, duration, etc., through the system of tense and aspect, there is a further, vital element of verb meaning carried in the semantic components of the verb itself.

Let us compare, for ease of reference, the verbs *hit, play, think* and *understand*. Only *hit* describes single transitory events. *Play* could refer to either events as in '*play* a note' (music) or series of events '*play* a game'. 'To *play*' (intransitive) has an element of duration. *Think* is, to some extent, timeless (although a thought is an event in itself). *Understand* describes a state, and is timeless in terms of specifying when it began or might end. *Hit* and *play* both seem to be restricted with reference to time – beginning and ending. *Think* could be either restricted or timeless, depending on the permanence of meaning. Thus there are important semantic components in verbs which have grammatical consequences, usually in the form of a restriction as to the tense they can be phrased in. The case of 'understand' is a little more complex. To say 'I understand what you're saying' would be regarded as acceptable – in fact, it might even be regarded as the 'normal' way of using 'understand' in the present. To say 'Today, I am understanding . . .' might raise a few eyebrows – but it could be argued that the present progressive captures well the temporary, transitory meaning of 'understand'. After repeated failure to understand, now the speaker understands, but not certainly – there is doubt.

This case raises the possibility that for a learner of English as a second or foreign language, unnecessary prescriptions are coded in the grammar, denying the possibility of creative use that a mother tongue speaker may have. 'Are you liking England?' asks an English person of the visitor from overseas. 'Oh yes I'm liking it a lot', replies the visitor. Acceptable or not? [See Leech (1971) and Bland (1988) for interesting discussions of this issue.]

TASK

Comment on the use and meaning of the verbs in the text which follows, written by a second language learner.

> <u>Shopping in a market is very different</u>
> <u>from shopping in a supermarket</u>

Man has to go to the market for buying essential things for his daily life. There are two types of market such as local or street market and supermarket. Local or street market is always very ɪ᷒ crowdy and noisy and also dirty. ~~the~~ Different commodities are found in scattered places. Everything is placed in happazard way, price of the ~~com~~ things vary from one shop to another. There is scope for barganing. Quality of goods are not up to the mark. Shopkeeps sometimes ~~sale~~ sell their goods through hawking voice. Method of service is not appreciable.

On the other hand, supermarket is calm & quiet and also neat and clean. Different varieties of goods are available in a particular place. Everything is kept in a systematic order, price is reqsonable and fixed, there is no scope of barganing but people can buy the commodities through their own choice. Quality of the things are also better. Behabiour and method of service is appreciable.

Considering above facilities in supermarket I believe that supermarket is a suitable place for ~~markes~~ shopping of all stages of people.

ACTIVITY 2.10

Aim   This activity examines the way verbs in the present tenses behave.

A)   Study the following sentences and comment on the meaning of the verbs in the present tenses in each example. What different meanings do you find?

1)   'Let my son's death be a lesson', says mother.
2)   He knows six languages.
3)   Plutonium is a highly volatile substance.
4)   'Lineker shoots! It hits the post!'

5)   I say that you're wrong.
6)   She wakes at seven.
7)   'If you live here you are treated like rubbish.'
8)   LABOUR TRIES TO REVIVE KINNOCK (newspaper headline).
9)   He's suffering from a sore throat.
10) You're imagining things.
11) 1941: Hitler Invades Russia.
12) The competition sponsors are offering a chance to see Michael Jackson in London.
13) DO NOT SIT ON THE TABLES. THE LEGS ARE BEING BROKEN (notice).

B)   For each of the examples above, make an assessment of how far into the past and the future each of the utterances refers. Try to map it onto a time line. For example: 'He likes to get up early' – 'likes' refers to some sort of routine or fairly stable set of affairs/habit – a state. It has its origins in the past (indefinite), and there is no reason why it will not carry on in the future.

   We could represent the example sentence visually (Figure 2.3).

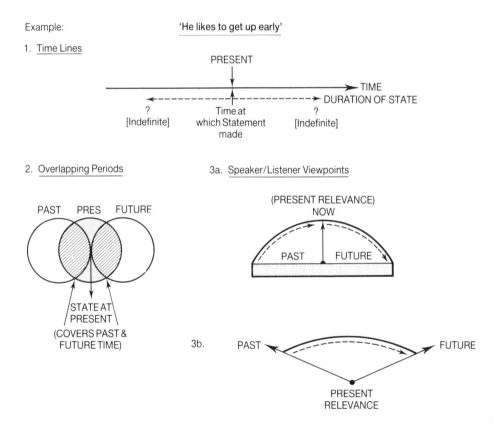

FIG. 2.3 'He likes to get up early.'

Thinking questions

Do you think that the verb tense tells us about time itself, or about the way the speaker/writer sees time? How far must we assume that speaker and listener share the same conventions regarding the expression of time when trying to interpret verb meaning?

TASK

Read through the following text and answer the questions. Do the uses of the present tenses in the text conform to the meanings you have established in this activity? Check your findings against the relevant sections in a reference grammar.

Bard 'is too tough for today's pupils'

by GUY FLEMING

SHAKESPEARE and Dickens *have been branded* as too difficult by some Devon secondary schools.

Now they *are considering* switching to another examining board so students would not have to study the classical authors for English GCSE exams.

Teachers elsewhere in Britain have already said they will withdraw pupils from examinations because the youngsters *can't* cope with texts such as Romeo and Juliet or Great Expectations.

Some teachers *claim* the set texts, central to the back-to-basics drive by Ministers, are well beyond the abilities of too many pupils and that, with only weeks to go before the examinations, they have not had enough time to prepare.

The original set texts were intended to test the reading skills of pupils of average ability and above.

The choices had been seen as a victory for traditionalists.

Devon's senior education officer Valentine Dubuisson said he *was* aware discussions were taking place – but as yet no schools in Devon had decided to switch examining boards.

Ken Watson (Con, Ashburton and Buckfastleigh), chairman of Devon's education committee, said the ability of pupils to master the great classics had been underestimated for many years.

He said 'I would be very sorry to see them disappear from the GCSE syllabus. A lot of it *has to do with* the quality of the teaching.'

Plymouth's Howard Davey (Lab, Trelawney) said he *was in favour* of broadening the range of set books to include neo-classical and modern works, provided that the 'mix' was evenly spread.

He said: 'I think it is also important to adopt a less dull approach to learning.'

Today a spokeswoman at Southway Comprehensive said the school had not even considered withdrawing pupils.

'Classical literature is part of our rich heritage,' she said. It '*reflects* our culture. Our Head of English *is satisfied* with the new curriculum. We *believe* in a mix of old and new. Our pupils are well able to cope.'

The examining board for South West schools is the Northern Examination Association which *follows* Government requirements.

The present syllabus *is* still experimental until next year after which there can be no opting-out.

Schools that withdraw pupils would have to switch to an alternative examining board which *does not include* classic literature (*Plymouth Evening Herald*, 21 May 1992).

Please refer to the verbs *italicized* in the text.

1) Lines 1–2: when did this happen?
2) Line 4: how do we know this is likely to stop soon?
3) Line 11: what is the time reference (*past, present* or *future*)?
4) Line 14: why present simple here?
5) Line 27: when was the education officer 'aware'?
6) Line 39: is this a present time reference?
7) Line 42: is Shakespeare still in favour (at the time of the report)?
8) Lines 54, 55, 56 and 61: why use the simple present here?
9) Line 63: will this state continue?
10) Lines 68–69: does this examination board exist at the time of writing?

ACTIVITY 2.11

Living in the past
Aim   This activity explores the ways in which the past tense in English works.

A)   Comment on the differences in meaning between each of the following pairs of sentences. Create a context for each sentence in the pair of utterances in order to assist you in distinguishing the meanings. From doing this exercise, what do you find out about the way in which English expresses past time?

1) A. That room is empty.
    B. That room has been empty for ages.
2) A. I have been studying your report.
    B. I have studied your report.
3) A. Someone stole my bicycle.
    B. Someone has stolen my bicycle.
4) A. All my friends have seen *Dances with Wolves*.
    B. All my friends saw *Dances with Wolves*.
5) A. I solved the problem.
    B. I had solved the problem.
6) A. I was sick.
    B. I was being sick.
7) A. I jumped.
    B. I was jumping.
8) A. Harry fainted.
    B. Harry used to faint.
9) A. I have eaten many different types of food.
    B. I would eat many different types of food.
10) A. The thief was being beaten up.
    B. The thief had been beaten up.

B)   Try to represent selected examples from the set above visually, illustrating which time references are transitory, which references are more continuous in nature, and which have a link to the present. Try different ideas. Which of your ideas do you think is most effective? (Refer to the examples of conceptualizing time on p. 53).

Thinking question
How much overlap between present and past time do you perceive by looking at the ways in which the English verb system expresses present and past time?

Further ideas

Time references
A major problem with English is that there is no one-to-one correlation between verb tense and time. The choice of verb form to express a particular state of affairs or activity depends on the speaker's perception of time and when the state of affairs or activity begins or ends. Thus, because English speakers use the simple present tense, it does not mean they are talking exclusively about time now. The context of use is critical for full understanding. So also is a knowledge of 'special uses' of English tenses for effect. How, for instance, does a listener or reader interpret the following?

'You'll be amazed by a Mazda' (commercial). Is it future? (will?) or is it present (the listener can actually see the car)? Or is it deliberately ambiguous in order to create its effect on the listener/receiver? Will this only happen when you buy the car? Is it 'potential'?

'You'll be pleased to know that we're giving you a raise' (manager to subordinate). When is the listener supposed to feel 'pleased'? When is the raise coming? Now or in the future?

'I wanted you to know how I feel'. When did the person 'want'? Some time, unspecified, in the past? Or, for some reason, now? Has the speaker already said how he or she feels? Or is this an announcement that he or she is about to say how he or she feels?

You might like to try to identify further examples in English of this idea. More often than not, there are other time references – clock, day, date, month, items like 'today', etc., duration expressions – to anchor the speaker/listener's perceptions. Choice of particular tenses, aspects and forms gives us insights into a speaker's motives and attitude (e.g., distancing themselves from events by use of past forms or by giving events current relevance).

Thinking question
Comment on the following quotation on the basis of what you have found out
in these activities.

> In the past simple, 'in all cases the speaker conceptualises the action as *factual*,
> but with an element of *remoteness*' (in time or personal relationship) (Lewis,
> 1986: 74).

TASK

Read the text which follows and answer the questions. Do the uses of the past
tense conform to those you have already established? Check your findings against
a reference grammar.

1) Write a chronology of Sasportas' life, identifying the main *events* and *incidents*
   and, if possible, the dates on which these occurred. Enter your findings on a
   lifeline like the one below.

   BORN

   DIED

2) List all the activities in which Sasportas was engaged. What tenses are used?
   Why?
3) What events of his life will live on after Sasportas' death? What are the verb
   tenses/aspects used? Why?
4) Show the relationship between Sasportas' life activities and what lives on
   after his death in a diagram.
5) From your reading and analysis, what is the function of an obituary? How
   do obituary writers exploit the verb system to fulfil this function?

Obituary

Howard Sasportas

Sign and psyche

Howard Sasportas, who has died aged 44, was an American-born teacher and writer in psychological astrology. The family originated in Spain, but along
5 with other Jews were banished in 1492. Some ultimately went to New England – where Howard was born. With tolerance under Cromwell in the 17th century, another ancestor,
10 Jacob Sasportas, became London's first Rabbi.

Howard Sasportas arrived in London in 1973 to complete his Masters degree in psychology from
15 Antioch University, New York. In 1979 he received the Gold Medal from the London-based Faculty of Astrological Studies. With his friend and colleague, the Jungian analyst
20 Liz Greene, he established a training school, the Centre for Psychological Astrology, the only one in the world to unite the study and practice of astrology with counselling psychotherapy.
25   His own writings on the philosophy and psychology of astrology – including The Twelve Houses, The Gods of Change: Pain, Crisis and the Transits of Uranus, Neptune and Pluto, and
30 The Sun Sign Career Guide – have become classics in their field, as have his works with Liz Greene, among them The Development Of Personality and The Dynamics Of The
35 Unconscious.

He founded Penguin's Contemporary Astrology Series, Arkana, acting as midwife for many authors' work, and his teachings have become known
40 in Europe, Australia and the US.

In his work, he always found time to help students or colleagues, but outside his professional life, his countless friends will remember him more for
45 himself – his energy, adventurous spirit and courage in the face of difficulty – than just for his work. He was deeply spiritual and aware of the psychology of human nature and even after two
50 major back operations to correct a congenital spinal disorder, which eventually crippled him, he remained an inspiration to all.

Erin Sullivan

Howard Sasportas, born April 12, 1948; died May 12, 1992. (*Guardian*, 20 May 1992).

ACTIVITY 2.12

Back to the future

Aim   This activity explores the ways in which English expresses future time.

A)   Examine the sentences which follow and comment on what each one tells you about the way the future is expressed in English. How *definite* is the speaker about the future action, event or state in each case?

1) I'll go mad if the TV isn't turned off.
2) The match kicks off at 2.30.
3) She's about to drive off.
4) We're eating at seven this evening.
5) I will have been working here for one year by the end of December.
6) Morrow wouldn't have written it if he'd known.
7) How about a drink?
8) I'll be on my way then.
9) You'll be hearing from my solicitor.
10) He's getting married next year.
11) It's going to be a long, hot summer.
12) Let there be happiness.
13) Accidents will happen.
14) I won't be long.

B)   Try mapping the verbs in each of the above examples onto a diagram. What do you discover about the relationships between past, present and future as expressed by these verbs?

Thinking question
How far and in which ways are speakers expressing their opinions and attitudes when they talk about the future? How does this manifest itself in English?

TASK

Examine the texts A, B and C and answer the questions. How far does the way in which the future is expressed in each text conform to the ideas you have already assembled regarding the future?

A. Scotland will be dry and very warm. South-west England will have generally well broken cloud and sunny spells but with a chance of a few thundery showers. Northern Ireland, Wales and the rest of England will be mainly dry with plenty of sunshine but with a small risk of an isolated thundery shower later in the afternoon and evening. Freshening easterly winds will keep exposed coasts cooler than inland.

● **Outlook for Thursday and Friday**: Dry and sunny in the north, but turning increasingly showery in the south with a risk of thunder. (*Guardian*, 26 May 1992).

B. A warm and humid day across the country, although with a brisk easterly breeze eastern coastal areas will be cooler and fresher.

Showers will develop during the day and isolated thunderstorms are expected during the afternoon, with the areas greatest at risk being Wales, Northern Ireland and central and north-west England. Scotland is likely to see the best of the sunshine, although scattered thunderstorms may develop over the mountains later in the day.

● **Outlook**: Remaining very warm and humid generally with further outbreaks of thundery rain, although Scotland will remain mainly dry. (*Guardian*, 27 May 1992).

C. For much of England, Wales, Northern Ireland and southern Scotland it will be a fairly cloudy day with some rain which is likely to be heavy and thundery, especially over Northern Ireland, Wales, the Midlands and the south-east.

There may be some mist along southern and eastern coasts. The rest of Scotland and south-west England should have a dry day with sunshine at times.

● **Outlook for Saturday and Sunday**: Showery rain is likely over most parts (*Guardian*, 28 May 1992).

1) Which forecast is the most, and which the least, certain? Give your reasons focusing, in particular, on the verbs in each forecast. Note other features of the language which provide clues as to the forecaster's certainty, or otherwise?
2) What is the effect of the clauses beginning 'although' and 'but' in each forecast? What do they do to the verbs' meanings?
3) Which *outlook* is most certain?
4) Why do you think there is no reference to previous weather patterns in each daily forecast?

ACTIVITY 2.13

Aim To review uses of verbs in English and to examine the organisation of a text which spans a wide time range.

Read through the text and answer the questions which accompany it. Questions 2–9 inclusive refer to the italicized text.

Fishermen survive six months adrift

Reuter in Auckland

Two starving fishermen *have survived*[2] six months adrift at sea in a small dinghy, living off fish and rain water, the New Zealand Herald reported [5] yesterday.

If verified, it *would be*[3] the longest recorded voyage adrift at sea *surpassing*[4] 119 days spent by three New Zealanders and an American in an [10] upturned trimaran off New Zealand in 1989, the newspaper said.

The two men, Tabwai Mikaie, aged 24, and Arenta Tebeitabu, aged 40, from the remote South Pacific nation [15] of Kiribati *were found*[5] on a beach in Western Samoa after 175 days adrift, the newspaper said. They were washed ashore at the eastern end of Upolu Island *days after a 47-year-old col-* [20] *league died of starvation.*[6]

'I *have seen*[7] them. They *are*[7] just skin and bones. According to the doctors, they *will be*[8] in hospital for quite some time,' the Western Samoan police [25] commissioner, Daniel Galuvao said.

Their 13-foot dinghy *capsized*[9] in a cyclone and lost its outboard motor, but the men later *managed*[9] to right the boat.

[30] They *drifted*[9] more than 900 miles out to sea and away from the Kiribati island of Nikunau, southeast of Western Samoa, police said.

The men *survived*[9] by catching fish, [35] including sharks. (*Guardian*, 15 May 1992).

Questions

1) Read through the text and count all the references to *past, present* and *future* time:

Past   =
Present =
Future   =

Total   =

2) Why not say 'survived'?
3) What time period is being referred to here – past, present or future?
4) Why does this have a 'present' structure '*-ing*'?
5) Could the writer say 'have been found'?
6) How many time references in 'days after . . . starvation'?
7) What is the connection between these two verbs?
8) How sure is the speaker?
9) Which of these four verbs describes a specific incident?

Thinking question
Are there any other clues as to time in this text, apart from the verbs?

ACTIVITY 2.14

Verbs and narrative sequence
The sentences which follow create a story but, as they appear below, they are mixed up. Your task is to arrange them in an appropriate order to make a story.

A young man is explaining how he has lost his fiancée . . .

I feel lonely and miserable.
I wouldn't have done that if I'd actually known.
But I know she won't do that.
I was going to try and cheer her up.
I've started learning a new language — to try and keep my mind off her.
She was feeling low, depressed.
I would give up if I didn't have so many good friends.
I suppose I'll never see her again.
She screamed at me and hung up the phone.
I'm feeling really miserable today, as you can see.
I'd tried just about everything, but I still couldn't make her realize.
I just wish she'd call me.
By the end of the month, it will have been six months since I last saw her.
I wanted to see her to sort it out.
My class starts at 8 this evening.
I phoned her to try and explain how I felt.
She'll probably end up marrying someone else now.
I haven't seen her for so long.
I stood there and cried. I knew it was over.

Thinking questions
1) Consider how your knowledge of the system of tenses and aspect in English helped you to arrange the sentences in an appropriate and meaningful manner.
2) Consider what other knowledge — linguistic and knowledge of the world — helped you to arrange the sentences.
3) Comment on any connections between grammar and narrative sequence, as exhibited in the story you have created.

TASK

Arrange the events and incidents in the text in Activity 2.13, 'Fishermen survive six months adrift', in their *chronological* order, from the very first to most recent.

Why do you think that newspaper reports often present events in an order different from the one in which they actually occurred?

ACTIVITY 2.15

State or event?

1) Study the list of verbs which follows and divide them into *three* groups, depending on whether you think they can only be used to describe actions, states (simple verb forms), or only used to describe events (progressive or continuous verb forms) or can be used for both. Make up examples from the list to help you sort it out. Complete a table like the one below by entering the verbs in the appropriate columns.

| be   live   love   change   get   stay   seem   ache |
| hit   have   come   impress   pass   know   build   deserve |

State	Event	State/event

If you use the verbs in the past simple tense, does this change the categorization you have created? Can you explain your findings?

2) Comment on the differences in meaning, if any, between the pairs of sentences below. Create contexts in order to clear up any potential ambiguities.

1) A. He's an idiot.
   B. He's being an idiot.
2) A. I'm having difficulty.
   B. I have difficulty.

3) A.   I think of you day and night.
    B.   I am thinking of you day and night.
4) A.   My elbow hurts.
    B.   My elbow is hurting.
5) A.   I'm depending on you.
    B.   I depend on you.
6) A.   She's sick
    B.   She's being sick.

Thinking questions
1) How significant is the state/event difference for the second language speaker of English? Would lack of knowledge of this concept lead to errors in usage?
2) Is the state/event distinction a component of a verb's meaning that a learner would find useful?

Further ideas

Other ways of talking about time

Verbs are central components of English, both grammatically (a sentence needs a main verb in order to conform to conventional grammatical descriptions) and semantically (verbs carry lexical and notional meanings about such categories as 'movement' and 'time'). Texts stripped of verbs make little sense as we saw earlier in this section. However, to put the weight of time on the verb and only the verb may be unfair. English has many ways of expressing time apart from the verb itself. (As confirmation of this, go through any of the texts so far included in this chapter to find other ways in which time is dealt with.)

Perhaps we need to look at the question of time and reality with a broader view than is traditionally accepted by grammarians? For example, was it the verb tenses which helped you construct the chronology of the text in the task in Activity 2.13 (p.61) or was it a combination of factors? What do you think? Does this imply we should stop teaching verbs and any other grammatical item as items alone? Or should we be approaching language with a concept of 'slices' of meaning, which forms enable us to transmit? In other words, grammatical classes are a means, not an end in themselves.

TASKS

A)   Compare the following extracts from well-known reference grammars. Note differences between them. Which do you prefer and why?

States and events

A. **104**

Since tense relates the meaning of the verb to a time scale, we must first give some attention to the different kinds of meaning a verb may have. Broadly, verbs may refer either to an EVENT (*i.e.* a happening thought of as a single occurrence, with a definite beginning and end), or to a STATE (*i.e.* a state of affairs which continues over a period, and need not have a well-defined beginning and end).

Thus *be, live, stay, know, etc* may be considered STATE VERBS, and *get, come, leave, hit, etc* EVENT VERBS. This distinction is similar to the distinction between count and mass nouns, and (as we saw in . . . for count and mass), it is to some extent a conceptual rather than a real distinction. The same verb can change from one category to another, and the distinction is not always clear: *Did you remember his name?* could refer either to a state or to an event.

To be more accurate, then, we should talk of 'state uses of verbs' and 'event uses of verbs'; but it is convenient to keep to the simpler terms 'state verb' and 'event verb'.

105

The distinction between 'state' and 'event' gives rise to the following three basic kinds of verb meaning (illustrated in the past tense):

(1)	STATE	Napoleon was a Corsican.
(2)	SINGLE EVENT	Columbus discovered America.
(3)	SET OF REPEATED EVENTS (HABIT)	Paganini played the violin brilliantly.

(Leech and Svartvik, 1975: 64)

B. **9.3 Stative and dynamic verbs**

Some verbs are not generally used in progressive forms. They are called **stative** because they refer to **states** (e.g. experiences, conditions) rather than to actions. In a sentence like:

*She **loves/loved** her baby more than anything in the world.* Loves (or *loved*) describes a state over which the mother has no control: it is an involuntary feeling. We could not use the progressive forms (*is/was loving*) here.

Dynamic verbs, on the other hand, usually refer to **actions** which are deliberate or voluntary (*I'm making a cake*) or they refer to changing situations (*He's growing old*), that is, to activities, etc., which have a beginning and an end. Dynamic verbs can be used in progressive as well as simple forms. Compare the following:

progressive forms	**simple forms**

1 Dynamic verbs with progressive and simple forms:

I'm looking at you.	*I often look at you.*
I'm listening to music.	*I often listen to music.*

2 Verbs which are nearly always stative (simple forms only):

—	*I see you.*
—	*I hear music.* [...]

3 Verbs that have dynamic or stative uses:

deliberate actions	**states**
I'm weighing myself.	*I weigh 65 kilos.*
I'm tasting the soup.	*It tastes salty.*
I'm feeling the radiator.	*It feels hot.*

Stative verbs usually occur in the simple form in all tenses. We can think of 'states' in categories like [...]

1 Feelings:	*like, love*, etc.
2 Thinking/believing:	*think, understand*, etc.
3 Wants and preferences:	*prefer, want*, etc.
4 Perception and the senses:	*hear, see*, etc.
5 Being/seeming/having/ owning:	*appear, seem, belong, own*, etc.

Sometimes verbs describing physical sensations can be used in simple or progressive forms with hardly any change of meaning:

   Ooh! It **hurts!** = *Ooh! It***'s hurting.**

Can/can't and *could/couldn't* often combine with verbs of perception to refer to a particular moment in the present or the past where a progressive form would be impossible [...]

   I **can smell** *gas.* = I **smell** *gas.*

(Alexander, 1988: 160–1)

B)   Answer the questions on the short text which follows.

Weather watch : *Manna from Heaven*

Paul Simons

When the Children of Israel collected manna from heaven during their exodus from Egypt, did they experience a meteorological miracle?

5   One school of thought is that the manna was sticky sweet sap oozing out of the tamarisk, a shrub growing in the Wady Feiron, where the Israelites are believed to have camped. On the 10 other hand, there could be a bizarre meteorological explanation.

Showers of nutritious lichen are known to occur in the Middle East. Leconora esculenta is a rather flaky 15 lichen which easily peels off the rocks it grows on and blows around in the wind. There are several cases of people being showered with and eating it. In 1829, during the war between Prussia 20 and Russia, there was severe famine in a large part of the Caspian. One day, during a violent wind, the surface of the countryside became covered in the lichen. Seeing their sheep eat it, the 25 people ground the lichen down into flour and made bread from it.

There are other possible types of manna, but what causes them is a mystery. On March 13 1977, as Alfred 30 Osborne and his wife returned home from a church service, they heard a clicking noise. Suddenly hundreds of nuts fell from a practically clear sky, bouncing off cars (as reported in the 35 Bristol Evening Post March 14, 1977). It's even more puzzling where fresh ripe hazelnuts could come from in mid-March, as they don't mature in Britain until late summer.

40   But possibly the most exotic form of manna to fall to earth was a report from Kentucky in 1876 of a shower of meat over the backyard of a house. As reported in the local Bath County 45 News: 'Mrs Crouch was out in the yard at the time making soap, when meat which looked like beef began to fall around her. The sky was perfectly clear at the time, and she said it fell like large 50 snow flakes.'

The meat was apparently perfectly fresh and tasted of mutton or venison. (*Guardian*, 28 May 1992)

---

1) Underline all verbs in the text with *state* meaning.
2) Circle all verbs in the text with *event* meaning.
3) Compare 1) and 2) – what do you learn about verbs and time reference? Does anything contradict what you have so far found out about state and event verbs?

Verbs: patterns of structure

Aim   To examine key features of English verb structures.

ACTIVITY 2.16

Verb forms
Aim   To identify and classify different types of verb forms.

1)   Each of the verbs below is in the *base* or *infinitive* form. (This is the form you will find if you look the word up in a dictionary.) Write down the *simple past* form and the *past participle* of each verb in a table like the one provided. An example is done for you.
2)   Look at the patterns of past and past participle that the verbs possess. Try to put them into groups according to their similarities.
3)   Does there seem to be a consistent 'rule' for creating past forms and past participle forms in English? Look at the examples, and make up some rules as if advising a second language learner about how to form the past or past participle.

> pick   run   lift   drink   write   tell   analyse   read   cut
> draw   enjoy   pray   fly   cover   print   cook   polish
> bury   listen   play   drive   teach   learn   spell   hunt
> grow   mark   see   break

Infinitive	Past	Past participle
love *pick* *etc.*	*loved*	*loved*

Thinking question
Do you think a second language learner faces a grammatical problem (that is, a question of which 'rules' to apply) or a vocabulary problem (a question of new 'words') when trying to learn the past forms of English verbs?

TASK

List 20 English verbs which you think would cause problems for the learner of English as a second language when wanting to use past and past participle forms.

What strategies would you suggest for learners learning these verb forms?

ACTIVITY 2.17

Verb types
Aim To identify and analyse different verb types and sentence patterns.

A) Divide the set of sentences which follows into *three* groups according to what types of word or phrase follow the main verbs (*italicized*). Comment on their properties – grammatical and semantic.

1) He *becomes* miserable easily.
2) I *dislike* eating raw fish.
3) I *felt* I had failed.
4) I *couldn't let* him continue.
5) I *like* my coffee black.
6) Her bike *cost* her £200.
7) She *didn't arrive*.
8) Bill *cycles*.
9) He was *made* Foreign Secretary.
10) I *had* my house painted last week.
11) I *showed* him how to fix his bike.
12) I *gave* her the money I owed her.
13) She *doesn't like* him being rude.
14) The madman *ran* amok in the market.
15) He's a friendly sort of person.

B) Which of the verbs in the list which follows can not take a direct *object* (*intransitive*)? Which verbs need an *object* in order to be 'complete' (*transitive*)? *Example* He eats spinach [*transitive* use: spinach is the direct object] He eats to live [*intransitive* use: no direct object]. Which verbs can be used in both of these ways?

look	seem	grow	make	go	enjoy	jump	smell	run
turn	have	appear	risk	sound	become	be	get	

C)   All the verbs which follow are verbs of 'saying'. Are they transitive or intransitive or both? Compose example sentences to demonstrate your points.

> admit   command   suggest   promise   order   offer   shout
> persuade   propose   deny   agree   argue

TASKS

1)   List the grammatical properties of English verbs you have encountered in Activities 2.16 and 2.17.

Thinking questions

When learning a new verb in English, how much grammatical and other (semantic) information does the learner need to acquire about the verb itself – its components of meaning – at the time of learning the verb? Is there such an entity as a 'regular' verb in terms of grammatical/semantic properties? If so, what are the properties of these verbs? How can a teacher help a learner to master the different types of verb?

2)   Look at the list of verbs which follow. They all refer to ways of movement by people on foot. In what ways are you able to distinguish between the different meanings? List the factors – for example, speed of movement – which help distinguish the meaning of one from another.

> stroll   amble   stride   swagger   limp   strut   saunter   march
> trip   mince   prance   stump   plod   totter   pace   waddle
> stagger   trudge

Thinking question

Are there other semantic aspects of English verbs which have grammatical implications? (It may help to distinguish between purely semantic characteristics of verbs, as illustrated in the task above, and semantic components which have grammatical consequences, such as whether the verb takes an object transitivity or describes a state or event tense and aspect.) [Examples include the verb 'develop', which may pose a transitivity problem, and 'weigh' or 'am' which may give problems as to use with different tenses and aspects of the verb: simple and progressive.]

ACTIVITY 2.18

'To look or looking? That is the question'
Aim   To examine the problem of infinitive and participle forms in English.

A)   If Hamlet had begun his famous speech 'Being or not being, that is the question . . .' instead of the immortal 'To be or not to be . . .', would the meaning have been altered in any way?
B)   Divide the list of verbs below into three groups, as follows:

1) Verbs which can only be followed by an '-*ing*' form, e.g., 'I enjoyed *eating* the local food'.
2) Verbs which can only be followed by a '*to*' form, e.g., 'I want *to go* out'.
3) Verbs which can be followed by either an '-*ing*' or a '*to*' form, e.g., 'I like *to eat/eating* the local food wherever I go'.

Compose sentences to illustrate your findings.

> practise   hate   decide   make   forget   prefer   try
> remember   intend   agree   hope   doubt   consider

Do you see any differences in meaning in the type 3) patterns between the '*to*' form and the '-*ing*' form, as in 'I like eating' and 'I like to eat'? Use any examples you find during the exercise.

Thinking questions
Is the choice of the infinitive or the '-*ing*' form in English a question of meaning or of structure? Are there any set patterns with specific meanings using either the '*to*' or the '-*ing*' forms of the verb? Do certain verbs have a restriction as to the nature of the items which follow them?

Further ideas

Components of verbs

There are five basic components of the verb in English (Figure 2.4):

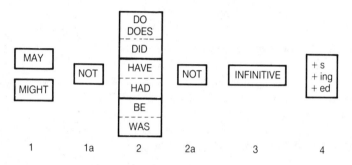

FIG. 2.4 The building blocks of verb groups.

- The basic form of the verb is the infinitive '*to* + verb' (e.g., to eat) (3).
- The basic form of the verb acts as the present simple tense (with '*-s*' or + -'*es*') for third person he/she/it) (4).
- The basic past form of the verb is '*-ed*', although many English verbs are notoriously irregular (past simple) (4).
- Aspects are formed by use of auxiliaries (*be, have*) and the participle forms ('*-ing*', '*-ed*') in various combinations (2 and 4).
- The auxiliary *do* is used for question forms in the simple tenses and negative forms in these tenses. Interrogative negative forms with other aspects are created around the appropriate parts of the auxiliaries (2 and 1a/2a).

What combinations can you make using the elements shown in Figure 2.4? For example, 1 + 1a + 2 (*have*) + 3 + 4 (*-ed*).

Transitivity restrictions

Every main verb in English has what we will term 'transitivity restrictions'. Some verbs are INTRANSITIVE – do not take a direct object; some are TRANSITIVE – take a direct object; and some can be used in both ways. e.g. *develop*.

1) I am developing.
2) I am developing a plan.
3) I am developing into a linguist.
4) I am developing to deepen my understanding.

Of these examples, only 2) has a transitive meaning. In the other examples, the meaning is intransitive – it could even be claimed that it is 'reflexive', in that there is an implication, especially in 3) and 4) that self-development may be taking place.

Sentence patterns

A variety of patterns are possible after the main verb in an English sentence.

Examples
1) I am having *second thoughts.*
   VERB   + OBJECT
2) I am   *very bored.*
   VERB + COMPLEMENT
3) I ate   *hungrily.*
   VERB + ADJUNCT (Adverb)
4) I eat   *to live.*
   VERB + ADJUNCT (Infinitive (nonfinite) clause)
5) He likes   *living in the country.*
   VERB   + COMPLEMENT (-ing clause)

The variety of sentence patterns possible in English is illustrated in Quirk et al. (1972). The complexity and variety can pose problems for the non-native speaker learner of English, as well as a native speaker writer (in the latter case, it may be a question of over-choice).

TASK

Read the following text and answer the questions on verb forms that accompany it.

Common Complaints

Jet lag

This summer most travel companies are *offering* lots of last-minute bargains, some to exotic locations in unfamiliar places. People may, indeed, find that they have booked to go somewhere with only a hazy idea of its geographical location. The travel agent will readily say something about the weather *to be expected* – usually unremitting sunshine and warm water – but may be less willing to offer information about drawbacks. One important factor for the holiday traveller, who is unlikely *to be spending* more than two weeks away, is jet lag.

Anyone aged 60 or more will remember the surprise with which people discovered that travel by jet had disadvantages. Until the 1950s, intercontinental travel was a slow business: *crossing* the Atlantic by even the fastest of the great passenger liners took four or five days, with the ship's clock being put back one hour each day. Flying to Australia involved several overnight stops. Jet aircraft transformed schedules, *enabling* executives *to leave* London at breakfast time and *arrive* in New York or Boston in time for lunch while colleagues at home were catching the evening train home. Soon, however, these travellers began to find that this rapid transition upset their bodies and their minds. For the first few days after arrival, not only does the body want *to sleep* at its normal bedtime; it wants *to eat* at home mealtimes, empty its bowel and bladder at the usual times, and do its thinking while the sun is out at home – not in the middle of the night.

The severity of the symptoms of jet lag depends on location, not on distance. Someone who flies from London to Cape Town may cover twice the distance of a trip to the United States, but Cape Town is only two hours away on the international clock, whereas the Caribbean and Florida are five or six hours off. Most of us can adjust with little difficulty to a shift of two hours; but anything over five becomes more uncomfortable. Travel eastwards, when the day of travel is shortened, seems *to be* more upsetting than in the opposite direction. This may need *to be* taken into account when choosing a holiday destination.

People vary enormously in the extent to which jet lag upsets them. Those who need little sleep seem *to do* better than those who need their eight or nine hours every night. Standard advice is *to reset* your watch and to try to eat, sleep and socialise at local times from day one. If possible, bank some sleep before *travelling* and sleep on the plane. Alcohol makes things worse – few experienced travellers drink much on cross-Atlantic flights. Research workers have established that a brain hormone, melatonin, helps the readjustment process, but attempts *to use* this hormone as a treatment *to hasten* adjustment have proved disappointing.

What does seem to help is exposure to sunlight. Having arrived at your destination, spend as many of the daylight hours as possible out of doors, and awake – *sleeping* on the beach is no good. If your idea of a good holiday is sleepy sunbathing by day (medically inadvisable because of the harmful effects of strong sun on the skin) and lots of activity at night, choose your location with care. Pick one within two or at most three time zones of Greenwich and jet lag will be no problem.

Dr Tony Smith
(*The Independent on Sunday*,
12 July 1992)

1) Can you use the alternative form − infinitive or '*-ing*' − for the words *italicized?*
2) What does this tell you about the infinitive/'*-ing*' problem?

ACTIVITY 2.19

Finite or nonfinite verbs?
Aim To examine the meanings and uses of different verb forms at sentence and discourse level.

A)   Study the list of words which follows and place each one in as many lexical and grammatical classes as you can, with an example to illustrate each.

> watching   broken   cooked   boiled   viewing   learned   pickled
> laughing   printed   publishing   cooking   booked

B)   Into which word class (noun, verb, etc.) does each of the *italicized* words fall in the sentences below?

List the criteria you used when making your decisions about word class membership.

1) The *waiting* train had been in the station for hours.
2) The *washing* machine's broken down again.
3) *Flying* is a dangerous sport.
4) *Boring* students can be a problem.
5) She has some *challenging* things to say about language.
6) The *burnt* cakes smelt awful.
7) Is anybody *interesting* coming to the party?
8) We huddled together in the *cramped* space.
9) *Roped* together, we felt safe.
10) I was very *annoyed* by his behaviour.

C)   Identify the finite and nonfinite verbs in the sentences which follow:

1) She was unable to move, pinned to the icy ground.
2) He didn't wait to find out.
3) 'To know know know him is to love love love him and I do' (song lyric).
4) Walking home, she saw a strange sight.
5) All he wanted to do was rest.

Now rewrite the sentences below using a nonfinite clause in place of a finite clause where it seems appropriate, for example, 'The man who was tired fell asleep': 'The tired man fell asleep' *or* 'The sleeping man had been tired.'

1) The leg which was broken set quickly.
2) I ate up quickly and rushed out.
3) A splendid time has been guaranteed and I am sure they will enjoy themselves.
4) It was the right thing which she did.
5) While I was sleeping soundly, I dreamt I was on Mars.

What is the effect of changing from a finite to a nonfinite clause?

Thinking questions

Why would a writer or speaker choose to use a nonfinite clause or verb? Would the choice affect meaning in any significant ways?

Further Ideas

Information load and nonfinite verb use

Newspapers are short of space. A lot of information has to be packed into a certain size of space in the paper, within restrictions imposed by type size, etc. One important way in which subeditors can achieve this is by using the nonfinite verb form. For example:

1) The remains of defence which were tattered . . .

   becomes . . . The *tattered* remains of the defence

   The use of nonfinite verb forms enables a writer to provide more information in a limited space than the use of many clauses to say the same thing. There is, however, a risk of vagueness and ambiguity. For example:

2) We saw him *leaving* the pub.

   In this example, who was leaving the pub? 'him' or 'we'? The main analytical question is whether the nonfinite verb is substituted for a dependent or nondependent relative clause. Another example may help to clarify this:

3) A *broken* man . . .

Is this 'A man who had been broken' or 'A man, who had been broken, . . .'
The context will help a reader decide in most cases whether the relationship is 'adjectival' (dependent) or 'resultant' (nondependent).

The nonfinite verb or clause might obscure the meaning relationships between the different propositions in a sentence. Let's look at how this might occur:

4) *Drifting without maps*, the expedition got lost.

Is the meaning here 'The expedition, which was drifting without maps, got lost.'? or 'The expedition which was drifting without maps got lost.'? In other words, is the meaning

As a result of A (drifting without maps), B happened?
or   In the state of A (drifting without maps), B occurred?

Again, contextual clues will help the reader decide. The normally overt relationship between cause and result, or noun and descriptor are suspended by the use of the nonfinite forms. The reader has the task of grasping the meanings.

When you next look at a newspaper, check to see which patterns – dependent or nondependent; cause/effect – are dominant.

TASKS

1)   Identify the finite and nonfinite verbs in the text in Activity 2.18, 'Common complaints'. Then try to rewrite the text without nonfinite verbs. What is the effect of the rewriting on the text's meaning?

2)   Read through the extracts which follow and answer the accompanying questions.

A. Inside, under a neo-classical ceiling, where moments before traders were busily jotting numbers on pads, milling around stations that looked like giant bugs with their bevy of monitor screens, traders lined up cheek by jowl, reaching out to shake hands with Mr Gorbachev and Mr Reagan as they waded slowly through the throng.

B. As Mr Gorbachev, surrounded by a sea of faces looked up at the visitors' gallery, packed with photographers and TV cameramen, it was clearly a case of capitalism swallowing communism rather communism burying capitalism.

(*Guardian*, 14 May 1992).

1)   Identify the main verb in each sentence, and its subject in each case.
2)   Divide each sentence into a series of 'propositions'. Each proposition should be able to stand as a sentence in its own right. How many are there in each of the extracts? What grammatical devices has the writer used to create one sentence out of several propositions?
3)   Construct an 'information map' for each sentence (see Figure 2.5). What do the 'maps' demonstrate?

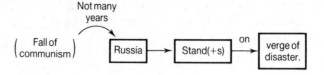

FIG. 2.5   An information map.

Example
Russia, not many years since the fall of Communism, stands on the verge of disaster.

Modals and modal meaning

Aim   To investigate the system of modal auxiliaries in English and examine its contribution to sentence meaning.

ACTIVITY 2.20

Write down as many ways as you can for the following:

1) Asking someone for permission to do something.
2) Requesting something from someone.
3) Imposing obligation on others.
4) Expressing the necessity for doing something.
5) Expressing the possibility of an event happening.

Note any similarities in the ways in which the different speech acts are expressed, in particular whether they feature a modal auxiliary (*can, may,* etc.), whether they are statements or questions, and whether they are positive or negative. Also, note ways in which they differ.

What conclusions do you draw from this activity with regard to the use of modal auxiliaries and the expression of different social functions of language in English?

ACTIVITY 2.21

The grid below relates various concepts and social functions in English to modal verbs. Put a tick where you think there is a correspondence between a verb (in the left-hand column) and a concept or social function (on the top). Make up an example sentence for every type of correspondence in order to check your ideas.

	certainty	possibility	probability	ability	obligation	necessity	doubt	permission	invitation	request	agreement	advice	warning
may													
can													
might													
could													
should													
must													
ought to													
have to													
be able to													
will													
shall													

Can you think of any further modal or verbal expressions which could be added to the set on the left of the table? Or any concepts or functions which could be added to the set on the top of the table? If so, add them and complete the table accordingly.

What are your conclusions about the relationship between the grammatical form and the function of an utterance after doing this activity and Activity 2.20? Comment on this relationship.

ACTIVITY 2.22

A)   Using your reference grammar, distinguish between ways of expressing *possibility, probability, certainty* and *ability* using modal auxiliaries. Are there any cases where there is *formal* overlap in expressing the meanings (where the same expression – e.g., *'may'* – is used for different purposes)? Can you express these relationships diagrammatically?

B)   What other ways are there of expressing the above concepts (possibility, etc.) apart from using modal auxiliaries? Suggest *one* alternative way of expressing each of the sentences without using a modal auxiliary. What is the meaning in each case?

1)   You can go skiing.
2)   Bill should organize his work better.
3)   You have to be more aware.
4)   I didn't know she could do maths.
5)   You may refer to a grammar.

C)   Do you agree with Leech and Svartvik (1975: 128, sect. 292) that there is a 'scale of likelihood'? And do you agree with Bolitho and Tomlinson (1980) that attempts to give these expressions a 'percentage certainty' (see ex. 2.12) are purely arbitrary?

Are there other ways of describing the differences between the meanings of the modal auxiliaries which express *likelihood* and *obligation*?

ACTIVITY 2.23

What differences in meaning between the following pairs of utterances can you see?

1)   A.   She could run very fast.
    B.   She was able to run very fast.
2)   A.   You mustn't smoke.
    B.   You don't have to smoke.
3)   A.   You should go.
    B.   You ought to go.
4)   A.   You needn't drive.
    B.   You don't need to drive.
5)   A.   I may walk.
    B.   I might walk.

6) A. I shall be there.
   B. I will be there.
7) A. He had to cycle to work.
   B. He would cycle to work.

ACTIVITY 2.24

A) Consider the effect of using different modal auxiliaries in the blanks in the following texts. Decide on the most appropriate ones to use.

1) Students — remember not to smoke in the classroom. They — be punished if they continue to do so.
2) You — buy Hormono: it — make your baldness a thing of the past.
3) Your family — check their hair in case of infestation by head lice. This is a common complaint and parents — not worry about its occurrence.

List the factors that helped you to decide on the most appropriate items to fill the blanks.
   Try to describe the function of each text now that you have filled the blanks. Can you express the same message without using a modal auxiliary, in each case?

B) What is the function of the question in each of the following exchanges? What conclusions do you draw about the relationship between modals and functions?

1) A: Can you lend me 50p?
   B: Certainly.
2) A: May I come in?
   B: If you wipe your feet first.
3) A: Might I ask you what the matter is?
   B: Nothing.
4) A: Would you shut up?
   B: Oh . . . sorry.
5) A: Should I go now?
   B: I'd wait a bit if I were you.
6) A: Will you tell me the name of the Brazilian President?
   B: I don't know, sir.
7) A: Must you do that?
   B: But I can't help it.
8) A: Could she pass, do you think?
   B: I'm not so sure.

9) A: Ought I to tell him?
   B: Wait a bit.
10) A: Would you come with me?
    B: I'm a bit busy just now.

Thinking questions

1) What do you understand by the notion of a speaker being 'direct'? What is the relationship between speaker directness/indirectness and the use of the various modal auxiliaries? Refer to the example sentences in Activity 2.23.

2) Do you think it is fair to say that the use of modal auxiliaries by speakers/writers is often a means of 'hedging', or avoiding issues, or even being dishonest? Refer to any of the texts included so far in this chapter and the example sentences in the Activity 2.23.

3) Why is it that many speakers of English as a second language have difficulty with the use of modal auxiliaries, despite their apparently straightforward nature structurally?

Further ideas

Modals refer to the future?

'All modal auxiliary verbs have a future reference.' How far is this true? When we are predicting, this is certainly the case. Based on our current state of knowledge, we make statements about what we think will happen in the future. Obligation, for example, seems to have both future and present and past reference. Obligation is based on 'historical' or 'social' precedent. 'You must do that' carries a reference to a future action, but the obligation is grounded in the present, and probably the past, too – although how long into the past is difficult to identify. Ability has past, present and future reference. There is an overlap of meaning with certainty in this instance. Ability is born of past actions; by indicating that a person *can* do something, we are also saying we are sure they have the ability to do it and so will succeed if they try.

Modals are closely bound up with social meanings

Being tactful can involve skilful use of the modal system in English. Often when speaking a foreign language we become aware that we are being too direct, and thus may appear to be rude. In English, misuse of the modal system can also convey this feeling. For example, 'You must give me that' is too face-threatening to be a polite request to borrow something. Tact and indirectness are expressed through the modal system as well as other means (e.g., using a question instead of a statement to allow the listener a chance to avoid an issue). Too much insistence on the overlap between modal verbs and social meaning may be misleading, however. The modals do carry aspects of the 'surface' meaning of many utterances. But all statements have modality in that they are expressing speakers' attitudes to the listener or a subject of conversation.

Choice

Choice of modal verb, or the way in which a statement is framed, can give strong indications as to the 'closeness' the speaker may feel to the listener in terms of social status or personal knowledge. It is a similar set of signals which enables us to distinguish between fact, conjecture, opinion and hypothesis. Our understanding of texts is to some degree bound up with these abilities. The crucial element is the element of choice of expression. The subtleties of English usage are well illustrated by the choice of modal auxiliaries. But this is only a beginning to a full understanding of how textual modality works. Your analysis of the letter in the task below will assist you in seeing how choice works, and how 'playing' with choice can create subtle changes of meaning in a text.

TASKS

A)   Read the text below and answer the questions that accompany it.

The Daily Telegraph

1 CANADA SQUARE   CANARY WHARF   LONDON E14 5DT

ENJOY NINE DAYS' ESSENTIAL FAMILY READING - FREE WITH THE DAILY TELEGRAPH.

Dear Reader,

   I have enclosed a voucher entitling you to eight copies of *The Daily Telegraph* and one of *The Sunday Telegraph*, absolutely free. Just **take** it along to your newsagent to claim your free newspapers. You **can** either collect them every day, or arrange to have them delivered to your home.

5   **Take up** our offer in the first week – starting Friday, September 11 – and *you will also receive two free Good Schools Guide supplements*, on the following Tuesday and Wednesday.

The supplements **will** include reports on over 100 of the top state and independent schools throughout the country. Each report **contains** the detailed information
10 you need when you are thinking about what kind of school **could be** right for your children.

During your nine free days, you **will** also have the chance to enjoy the superb range of special pages, magazines and supplements that are of special interest to anyone with a young family, including our highly acclaimed supplement *You and*
15 *Your Family*. I have enclosed a leaflet which tells you about all this in more detail.

You **may wonder** why we are making such a generous offer? We have found that this is the best way to convince people how informative, entertaining and lively *The Daily Telegraph* is – and what better time **could** there be to discover our excellent family coverage for yourself?

20   One million people are impressed enough to buy *The Daily Telegraph* every day. We hope you **will** be too. Why not give it a try? Your nine days' free papers **can** begin on any Friday from September 11 to October 2, running through until the following Saturday. Just fill in the voucher and take it to any newsagent to claim.

There's no catch. You **will** be under no obligation to buy even a single issue of
25 *The Daily Telegraph*. I hope you enjoy an extremely entertaining nine days' free reading.

Yours sincerely,

Marketing Director

P.S.   **In the unlikely event** that you **are unable** to redeem your voucher at your
30 local newsagent please telephone The Daily Telegraph anytime on 0272 244 704.

1) Lines 2 and 5: what is the *function* of the verb (take; take up) in each case?
2) Lines 3 and 21: are these 'cans' the same in meaning?
3) Lines 8, 12, 21 and 24: are there different meanings of 'will'?
4) Line 9: why use the present simple?
5) Lines 10 and 18: what is the force of 'could' in these examples? Do they have the same meaning?
6) Line 17: what does 'may wonder' mean?
7) Line 29: why negative forms here?
8) What is the main function of the letter? Are there other ways in which the writer makes his point, and fulfils his purpose without employing the modal system?

B)   Examine the ways in which different reference grammars and EFL coursebooks treat modality. Could you suggest any ways of improving the presentation in any one grammar or coursebook?

Passive voice

Aim   To investigate the use of the passive voice in English.

ACTIVITY 2.25

Comment on the following statements:

1) Scientific text is always written in the passive voice. That's because scientific text is factual.
2) The use of the passive in a sentence shows that the statement is 'official'.
3) My EFL students have difficulty in understanding the *concept* that lies behind the passive.
4) The passive is only used for particular social effects. It is not normally used in everyday colloquial English.
5) Not every active statement can be transformed into the passive. In fact, it might not be necessary to do this.

Thinking questions
Make a list of 'facts about the passive' based on your responses to the above statements.

What types of 'facts' do you find yourself developing? Revise and update these as you go through the activities which follow.

ACTIVITY 2.26

Comment on the effect of the use of the passive in each of the following sentences:

1) Jones was sent off in the second half.
2) MADE IN JAPAN.
3) Plenty of people are being promoted.
4) I was married in 1977.
5) Carbon monoxide is produced under elevated temperature conditions.
6) You've been reminded about punctuality before.
7) My friend has had her bike stolen.
8) Why are you shamed by your mistakes in English?
9) It is only to be expected of him.
10) It is believed that grammar teaching can help learners.

Thinking questions
What conclusions can you draw from this activity regarding the use of the passive voice in English? Do you wish to change any of your 'facts about the passive' in Activity 2.25 on the basis of the exercise?

ACTIVITY 2.27

Comment on the following pairs of sentences:

1) A.   I can't open the door.
   B.   The door can't be opened.
2) A.   The house is sold.
   B.   The house is being sold.
3) A.   I won't tell her again.
   B.   She won't be told.
4) A.   I have my correspondence typed.
   B.   I have my correspondence typed by her.
5) A.   The supplies came yesterday.
   B.   The supplies were brought yesterday.

ACTIVITY 2.28

Write the following newspaper headlines out in full, as far as you are able. What do you learn about the use of the passive from this exercise?

1) Pilots killed (cf Blaze kills 4).
2) Police pelted as illegal party broken up (cf Party-goers pelt police).
3) State of emergency declared.
4) Gulf pilots used drug banned in UK.
5) Men injected in plutonium tests.
6) Gun victims named.
7) Wallace injured as Irish lose.
8) Taylor's game suited to uncertainty.
9) Bush accused of 'pushing' arms.
10) President ousted after gun battle.

Thinking questions
1) On the basis of Activities 2.27 and 2.28, are there any other facts that you would add to your list in Activity 2.25? Are there any new facts you would add to the list? Are there, for example, instances of usage which are not 'true passives'?

2) Are there different conceptual meanings of the passive? Use the *agent/ action/patient* (object) conceptualization in order to explain the sentences in Activity 2.27 and the full sentences in Activity 2.28.

Further ideas

The choice between using active and passive voice is extremely complex. The choice is made more problematical by the widespread use of the passive in academic textbooks (many people associate the passive with a sterile, arid form of academic writing, devoid of meaning beyond objective reality). Thus the need to focus on the *patient/object* of an action rather than the doer. In science, we are interested in states, not people. The scientist must appear to keep out of the action. Similarly, legal, medical and political talk employs the device of 'distancing' the speaker from the action and appealing to some unnamed greater authority, although speakers don't have to be excluded, as in 'I was given a prize'.

In other words, use of the passive may indicate a writer's intention or style. It is a powerful organizing device in discourse and may be a means of identifying writer/speaker attitude. The missing actor may also contain a host of assumptions shared by interlocutors, e.g., 'The rubbish was cleared . . .'. The question is 'how' – by municipal workers? (OK for Britain) or by any other person? (OK for places without a refuse collection service.)

A further important feature of the use of the passive is the relationship between front and end weight of sentences (see Leech and Svartvik, 1975). The passive enables *patients* to be front loaded and therefore to be highlighted in listener/reader's consciousness. The addition of a 'by' phrase containing the *actor/agent* changes the balance, by introducing an end-loading. Leech and Svartvik claim that the weight of a sentence/grammatical complexity increases towards the end of the sentence. This correlates with new information in a text: 'a sentence is generally more effective (especially in writing) if the main point is saved up to the end' (Leech and Svartvik, 1975: 175, sect 423) and 'The general rule is that the most important information is saved up to the end, so that the sentence ends with a sort of climax' (Op. cit., 174). Hence it happens that the most comfortable distribution of information in a sentence (because of discoursal pressure) 'forces' a passive (Rutherford 1987:161).

TASKS

A) Examine the following extracts from reference grammars. Would you change either of them on the basis of your work in this section?

> A. When people in general are the agents, an **active** form of the verb is sometimes used instead, with 'you' or 'they' as the subject. 'One' is used as the subject in this kind of clause in formal speech or writing.
> *You* can't buy iron now, only steel.
> *They* say she's very bright.

> B. In fluent English, passives occur naturally and spontaneously, without a conscious change from 'active' to 'passive'. In fact, active equivalents would be hard to produce for sentences like *The origin of the universe will probably never be explained*. (Alexander, 1988: 243).

B) Refer to the extract in Activity 2.18 entitled 'Common complaints' and then answer the questions below:

1) Lines 23–25: who put the ship's clock back? Does it matter that we aren't told in the text?
2) There are remarkably few passive forms in this text. Can you offer any explanations?

C) Refer to the extract in Activity 2.10 entitled 'Bard "is too tough for today's pupils"' and then answer the following questions:

1) Lines 1–2: who 'branded' Shakespeare and Dickens 'difficult'?
2) Line 2: who 'intended' to test reading skills?
3) Line 28: 'Discussions were taking place'. Why not say who was involved in the discussions?
4) Line 35: who do you think 'underestimated' pupils?
5) Line 46: would an active form of 'spread' make any sense?

D) 1) Go over the texts in Activity 2.13 ('Fishermen survive six months adrift') and Activity 2.15 ('Weather watch'). Compare the ways in which the passive is used in each one. Cross-refer your ideas with the 'Further ideas' above.
   2) Find examples of the use of the passive in advertising. What is the effect of this particular use on a listener or reader?

Prepositions and phrasal verbs

Aim   To examine the group of verbs in English most commonly referred to as 'phrasal verbs'.

ACTIVITY 2.29

Comment on the following statements:

1) An advanced second language speaker of English uses phrasal verbs frequently, and with confidence. It is a mark of their fluency that they can.
2) Knowing phrasal verbs is really a question of vocabulary.
3) Colloquial English speech contains large numbers of phrasal verbs.
4) Phrasal verbs do not appear much in written English. They shouldn't, either – it's a sign of bad usage.
5) Phrasal verbs are more difficult to learn than any other area of English because English is the only language which has phrasal verbs.

Thinking question
What advice would you offer to the would-be learner of English regarding the learning of phrasal verbs on the basis of your responses to the statements above?

ACTIVITY 2.30

A)   What is the grammatical relationship between the verb (in *italic*) and the phrase (in **bold**) which follows it? Try to group the verbs according to the properties you identify. Describe your criteria for each group.

1) My brother *shouted* **at Eric.**
2) Eric *called* **on James.**
3) I *played* **along with their ideas.**
4) My brother *picked* **up James** at 3.15.
5) The rain *set* **back our plans** by a month.
6) He *looked* **at his watch.**
7) She *woke* **up her husband** at 6.00.
8) The keeper *let* **out the tiger.**

B)   Examine the verbs (in *italic*) in the sentences below and try to divide the sentences into two groups. What are your criteria?

1) They *left* their best player *out* of the team.

2) She's *getting on* very well with Jones at the moment.
3) I *don't approve of* that sort of behaviour.
4) In many countries, young men *are called up* at the age of 18.
5) The motorist *ran over* the cat.
6) He *got* a book out of the library.
7) Meteorites *burn out* in the Earth's atmosphere.
8) She's *knocking about* with a strange group.
9) The ship *was fitted out* in a matter of weeks.
10) He *kept rubbing in* the fact that I had made a mistake.

C) Divide the following verbs into groups according to their meanings. The verbs are in *italic* and the particles (adverbs or prepositions) are in **bold**.

In the example sentences, which of the two-word verbs seem to have two separate divisible components of meaning? Which meanings seem to be intensified by the addition of the particle? Which verbs only have separate meaning unrelated to their component parts?

1) I wish I could *stick* **at** a task.
2) The plumber said he could *fix* **up** the bath.
3) When he was in trouble, all his friends *rallied* **round**.
4) I *noted* **down** a few ideas on the back of an envelope.
5) She tried to *talk* her clients **round** but failed.
6) On holidays, all my friends *drop* **by**.
7) The police had never *come* **across** such a bizarre crime.
8) All the bargains were *snapped* **up** by 10.30.
9) It was foggy, and I wasn't able to *make* **out** the shape of the rock.
10) The big clubs have *signed* **up** all the good players.

Applying tests

1) Try placing an adverb (e.g., *quickly*) before the particle in each of the verbs above. Is the sentence correct grammatically? For example,

    She picked me up at six.
    She picked me *promptly* up at six.

2) Try replacing the object (or subject, if the verb is intransitive. Make the sentence passive, too) with a pronoun in each of the example sentences. What patterns do you notice?
3) Try making the verb passive, if it is active. Can this operation be carried out? What is its effect?
4) In the example sentences, which of the main verbs seem to have two separate components of meaning? Which verbs seem to be intensified by the addition of the particle? Which seem to have a composite meaning?

ACTIVITY 2.31

A)   Work systematically through the lists below. Prepare examples which demonstrate the structural properties and meanings of each of the items.

List A	*List B*
pull through	get away with
try out	look up to
give up	grow out of
cry off	drop in on
go off	hold on to
throw out	
show in	
let down	
pass out	
set out	

Be creative!

B)   Using the verbs in the column on the left, and the adverbs/prepositions on the right, make up different types of two-word verbs with different properties – structurally and in terms of their meanings:

pay	in
come	down
keep	on
dry	away
call	off
move	around
pass	over
set	back
hold	from
put	up

Make up five phrasal or prepositional verbs of your own, using main verbs and particles. Decide on the grammatical properties of the verbs and put them in example sentences to assist readers in guessing their meaning.

Summary: phrasal or prepositional verb? Factors to consider

Structure

1) The preposition in a prepositional verb must come before the prepositonal object.
2) If the object is a pronoun, it must follow the preposition in a prepositional verb.
3) An adverb can be placed between verb and preposition in a prepositional verb.
4) A prepositional verb accepts a relative pronoun, e.g., *whom* after the preposition.

Question

Can you form the passive from an active form of a phrasal verb?

Note   Different reference grammars use different terminology for distinguishing between items. Check at least two reference grammars against this summary.

Meaning

Some phrasal verbs retain the meanings of the individual elements of the phrasal verb, but many others do not. In some cases the particle *intensifies* the meaning of the verb. There are also numerous examples of polysemy. Phrasal and prepositional verbs cannot be distinguished on semantic criteria, however.

Further ideas

In the field of English SL/FL teaching, phrasal verbs (PVs) occupy an unfortunate place in the demonology of learners and many non-native speaker teachers as well. Like all languages, the growth of English depends on the growth of the lexicon. In different non-native forms, new phrasal verbs have evolved, to some extent dispelling the myth that phrasal verb mastery is something only mother tongue speakers can aspire to.

to cope up with	SEAE/SWAE
to stress on	SEAE/MalE
to fair out	IE
to discuss about	SWAE

(SEAE = Standard East African English; SWAE = Standard West African English; MalE = Malaysian English; IE = Indian English.)

The above are all PVs developed in different varieties of the language. One of the distinguishing features of a good speaker of English is his or her ability and range of PVs. (Cambridge Proficiency Examinations have traditionally focused on PVs.) The key question for the learner is whether they are to be treated as grammatical items, or as vocabulary with certain grammatical peculiarities.

Grammatical peculiarities would seem to offer the learner more scope. A factor that might assist is to comprehend the richness of the metaphor afforded by PVs – many are intensely 'visual' in their meaning and are probably best learned as units of meaning, together with a strong image (see Shovel, 1985).

TASKS

A) Study the texts which follow and answer the questions which accompany them.

Mike plunges in to save girl

A Devon man became a holiday hero when he saved a two-year-old girl from drowning in Portugal – even though he can hardly swim.
5 Mike Maddocks from Park Road, Exeter, was *walking alongside* a river in the Algarve when he saw the Portuguese youngster *fall into* the water.

As his wife, Jenny, and two friends
10 *looked* on, he *dived off* the steep bank and managed to bring her to safety.

Mike, 44, who *works for* the Royal Navy at its Countess Wear stores depot, admits he cannot swim very
15 well but that did not *put him off* taking the plunge.

'I didn't *think about* it really, I just *dived in* and *got her out*', he said.

'I *acted on* instinct I suppose, even
20 though I normally wouldn't even *go down to* the deep end of the swimming pool.

'When I *dived in* I still had my clothes on and a bag on my back, so
25 it was quite difficult to save her.

'Although the river was calm and clear, it was certainly quite a struggle as I had to go 20 to 30 feet along the bank before I could *get her out*.'
30 Despite Mike's bravery in rescuing the girl, he was not thanked by her parents.

'After we *managed to* haul her out of the water and made sure she was
35 breathing alright, she *went off back* to her parents at a nearby picnic area, but all I *got from* the parents was a wave,' said Mike.

Ironically, although he can hardly
40 swim, his wife Jenny won life-saving certificate at school (*Exeter Express and Echo*, 20 May 1992).

---

1) Decide which of the *italicized* verbs are *phrasal*, which are *prepositional* and which are *verb* and *adverbial phrases*.
2) Lines 18, 29 and 37: what is the meaning of *get* in each case?
3) Line 33: what is the grammatical relationship between *manage* and *to*?

Woman *sets up¹ con²* at guest house

A couple *conned*[3] a Plymouth guest house landlady into believing that they were visiting a sick relative – then fled without paying their £304 bill, a court [5] heard.

Plymouth Crown Court was told that former tattoo artist Brenda Clarke, 49, and Keith Frith, 36, of Tremayne Terrace, Widegates, Looe, won the [10] sympathy of landlady Linda Fleet, of the Santa Barbara guesthouse, Alma Road.

When she heard that they were visiting Frith's sick mother in hospital she [15] stalled their payments for 12 days.

The couple, using the false names David and Jane Legitt, finally asked to settle the bill last October. When Mrs Fleet *made out*[4] the bill for £304, [20] Clarke said she needed to go to the bank to *draw out*[4] some money, said Paul Rowsell, prosecuting.

'She told Mrs Fleet to *put on*[5] the toast ready for breakfast for their [25] return. But return they never did.

'Fortunately Mrs Fleet noted down the number plate of the Mini car that Clarke was driving and she was later arrested.

[30] 'During the 12 days at Santa Barbara, Clarke avoided settling the bill and kept on extending their stay, ultimately to 12 days.

'The landlady was fed with bulletins [35] about the deteriorating state of the man's mother's health.'

Clarke yesterday admitted *making off*[6] without payment. She was conditionally discharged for 12 months and [40] ordered to pay £304 compensation.

Frith, who was not charged with the above offence, admitted three offences of theft and one of burglary.

He was *put on*[7] probation for three [45] years and ordered to pay £60 compensation.

John Bush, defending, said: 'His life has been blighted by drink. He has accepted he's a social pest.' (*Plymouth* [50] *Evening Herald*, 24 April 1992).

1)   What is the meaning of 'sets up'?
2)   Look 'con' up in a dictionary. What does it mean?
3)   Is this a phrasal or prepositional verb? If so, what is the particle?
4)   Is the meaning of 'out' similar to these two examples?
5)   How do you 'put on' toast?
6)   Can you replace this with another word?
7)   Is this a phrasal verb?

C)   Collect phrasal and prepositional verbs (multi-word verbs) from the press, television, radio and people's everyday speech. Try to classify them according to whether or not they are prepositional or phrasal verbs. Don't forget the importance of the context in which they occur – watch out for specific jargon, for example, in sports.

Adverbs and adverbials

Aim   To examine the contribution of adverbials to text meaning.

ACTIVITY 2.32

Examine the sentences which follow and decide on the function of the *italicized* elements in each one. They all fall into the class of grammatical item known as adverbials. What do they add to the meaning of the sentence in each case?

1) She fell *rather heavily*.
2) I felt *such* a fool.
3) It was an *extremely* beautiful morning.
4) The bedrooms are *upstairs*.
5) They live *expensively*.
6) He missed the shot *completely*.
7) *Forty years ago*, life was very different.
8) I'll see you *next week*.
9) The high load managed to pass *under the bridge*.
10) She's *just* fallen over.
11) He played *really badly*.
12) I *normally* go to bed *before midnight*.
13) *Once upon a time*, there was a rich prince.
14) I'm going *to South East Asia for my holiday this year*.
15) She put all her belongings *on the back seat*.

Thinking questions
1) Can you create categories in which to place the italicized items from the sentences above?
2) Are there any rules for the use and construction of adverbials in English, for example, in the ordering of phrases? Refer to your reference grammar if you are unsure or require further information.

TASK

Try to distinguish between ways of talking about the *frequency* (how often?), the *duration* (how long?) and the *accuracy* (when?) of different time expressions.

ACTIVITY 2.33

Do you notice any grammatical restrictions on the *position* of an adverbial in a sentence? Can an adverbial be placed anywhere in a sentence? Explain the differences in meaning between the following pairs of sentences.

1) A. She played really well.
   B. She played well, really.
2) A. Officially, you're not allowed to do that.
   B. You're not allowed to do that officially.
3) A. Certainly, you can't do that.
   B. You can't do that certainly.
4) A. Technically, you're wrong.
   B. You're technically wrong.
5) A. Never had I seen such a mess.
   B. I had never seen such a mess.

ACTIVITY 2.34

1) Examine the texts in Activity 2.11 ('Obituary') and Activity 2.13 ('Fishermen survive six months adrift'). Go through the texts and eliminate all the adverbials. What types of information have you deleted from the texts?
2) Of the adverbials which you have eliminated, decide which are 'tied' in some way directly to the verb, those which qualify the meaning of the adverbials or modify adjectives with which they co-occur, and those which comment on the 'mood' of the text – such as 'hopefully' in the initial position in a sentence.

Further ideas

Adverbials carry large amounts of information which enable us to be more specific about events and actions that we are describing. We can describe time, place, manner and frequency very closely by using adverbials. We can compare with adverbials – 'more quickly than' – and we also express personal opinions with adverbials – 'without any doubt . . . .'. It is the personal-opinions quality that also enables speakers to be vague as well as very specific. Consider the difference between 'We hope to help you' and 'Hopefully, we'll help you.'

Check through the newspaper extracts in Activities 2.4–2.15 to find instances of adverbials being used to express personal opinions.

Adverbials enable speakers to express such concepts as time, certainty and obligation. Because adverbials have this capacity to modify the verb phrase meaning, their importance may be under-rated by grammars and textbooks. In order to explore this idea, look through the text 'Common complaints' (p. 74) and eliminate adverbials. Notice the effect of this operation on the text's meaning and coherence.

Nouns and their properties

Aim   To examine the grammatical and semantic properties of the word class 'noun'.

ACTIVITY 2.35

Study the list of words that follows:

1) Decide what sorts of *concept* each one entails – whether the word identifies something which can be touched or seen, or not touched or seen, for example. Put them into categories.
2) Distinguish the items in terms of their *grammatical properties*. Again, put them into groups. (Use terms such as *countable, uncountable* (or *count* and *mass*), *concrete, abstract*, etc.)

gang	variety	sunshine
person	wood	talk
hair	harm	shopping
water	cutlery	news
tiger	rubbish	advice
education	team	tobacco
problem	majority	honesty
government	sugar	experience
furniture	army	tennis

Thinking question
Can you find any link between the conceptual and grammatical properties of nouns on the basis of this activity?

ACTIVITY 2.36

What grammatical problems might be associated with the *italicized* items in the sentences which follow?

1) She's the *cream* of the crop.
2) The *talks* broke down at noon.
3) That'll put *hairs* on your chest!
4) He had a couple of *coffees* before lunch.
5) She is only testing the *waters*.

6) My *Africa* is not the same as yours.
7) The two *Davids* don't seem to be getting on so well these days.
8) She ran off into the *woods*.
9) *MAN UTD* WIN AT LAST.
10) The *team* has decided to call it a day.
11) He had a good *cry* after the match.
12) I can't stand her *cooking*.

Thinking questions

1) List the grammatical problems associated with nouns in English which have emerged from Activities 2.35 and 2.36.
2) Check your reference grammar for confirmation of your findings about these grammatical features and to find further information on these problems. Note any features which you have found while doing the exercises but which are not dealt with in the grammar.

ACTIVITY 2.37

In English, many nouns are not countable. However, English does have a way of referring to specific instances, examples or parts of uncountable entities. This activity aims to explore some of these.

Write down the following:

1) *Units* (for example, 'pieces') of sand, paper, glass, rubbish, mud, chess, research, advice, hope, co-operation, anger, evidence, news.
2) *Measures* (for example, 'buckets') of water, oil, work, difficulty.
3) *Kind* (for example, 'type') of wood, car, insect, bread, cake, behaviour, trick, thought.

Thinking question

What grammatical and semantic properties do the *unit*, *measure* and *kind* words share?

ACTIVITY 2.38

A) Distinguish between the meanings of the following pairs of sentences. What conclusions can you draw about the differences between them? What part does grammar play in the meaning in each example?

1) A. Many people died.
    B. Many of the people died.
2) A. Not many cars passed yesterday.
    B. Not many of the cars passed yesterday.

3) A.   A few friends turned up.
   B.   A few of the friends turned up.
4) A.   Much food was eaten.
   B.   Much of the food was eaten.
5) A.   A little money was left over.
   B.   A little of the money was left over.
6) A.   Not much oil is left in the North Sea.
   B.   Not much of the oil is left in the North Sea.

B)   Do you notice any differences between the meanings of the *italicized* parts of the following pairs of sentences? Comment on any that you find.

1) A.   *All diligent students* study hard.
   B.   *Every diligent student* studies hard.
2) A.   She gave a present to *each couple*.
   B.   She gave a present to *every couple*.
3) A.   You can eat *every food* you like.
   B.   You can eat *any food* you like.
4) A.   You can ask *either of my friends*.
   B.   You can ask *any of my friends*.
5) A.   He ate *all the bananas*.
   B.   He ate *every one of the bananas*.
6) A.   She enjoys *everything*.
   B.   She enjoys *anything*.
7) A.   He gave fifty pence to *all of the beggars*.
   B.   He gave fifty pence to *each of the beggars*.

Thinking question
Does this activity highlight any restrictions on the use of words like *all*, *both*, *any*, *every*, *each*, and *either* with 'count' or 'mass' nouns?

C)   Discuss the differences in meaning between the *italicized* items in the pairs of sentences which follow.

1) A.   She was a woman of *few* ideas.
   B.   She was a woman who had a *few* ideas.
2) A.   Large *numbers* of people assembled.
   B.   A large *number* of people assembled.
3) A.   *What's* wrong?
   B.   *What* a fool!
4) A.   *One* man's meat is another man's poison.
   B.   *One* man ate the loaf.
5) A.   *All* the population was ecstatic.
   B.   *The whole* population was ecstatic.

6) A.   *Any* fool can see the reason.
    B.   Have you *any* problems?
7) A.   *Lots* of people were there.
    B.   A *lot* of people were there.
8) A.   That's *some* suit you're wearing.
    B.   I'd appreciate *some* new clothes.

Thinking question

Are there any rules which govern the types of premodifier various nouns might take as in the example sentences above? For example, count and mass nouns?

ACTIVITY 2.39

Nouns and verbs in company

Look at the sentences which follow and choose the correct form of the verb, either singular or plural, from the *italicized* pair.

What grammatical problems do the sentences illustrate? (Are these related to the noun or the verb, or both?)

1) The audience *was/were* enormous.
2) My team *is/are* playing away today.
3) The vast majority *agrees/agree* with current policies.
4) The public *is/are* tired of waiting.
5) A vast number of people *has/have* applied for shares.
6) A large quantity of oranges *was/were* rotting in the sun.
7) The Stars and Stripes *was/were* fluttering proudly from the mast.
8) Many drinkers believe that German and Danish beer *is/are* tastier than British beer.
9) No money *has/have* been spent on repairs and maintenance.
10) No people of that nationality *comes/come* here.
11) Nobody *knows/know* what is happening.
12) Neither John nor May *is/are* coming today.
13) Either you or I *are/am* wrong.
14) Either your eyes or your ears *needs/need* examining.
15) Few of us *likes/like* what we have seen.

Thinking question

What rules for agreement between noun (subject) and verb does this activity illustrate? Try to write some of these rules down.

ACTIVITY 2.40

In the following phrases, identify the *head* or *main* noun, and any items which *premodify* (come before) the head and any which *postmodify* (come after) the head. What type of item does not premodify or postmodify the head?

1) a really tough-looking opponent
2) an idea advanced by Chomsky
3) something unusual about the light today
4) the new education legislation
5) two of my grammar books
6) anyone with the slightest bit of common sense
7) incredibly unseasonal weather patterns
8) a good old-fashioned row
9) an internationally acclaimed applied linguist
10) the Archbishop of Canterbury's hostage troubleshooter

Thinking question
What types of item premodify nouns and what types of item postmodify nouns? For example, adjectives – do they tend to pre- or postmodify?

ACTIVITY 2.41

Comment on the relations between the nouns in the phrases which follow, noting head words and pre- and postmodifiers. Which are the main, or 'head' nouns?

1) the bottom of the door
2) the forest's destruction
3) Halliday's position
4) the goals of science
5) the trees' destruction by the wind
6) a good night's sleep
7) Denmark's great run
8) the fight against hunger
9) the politician's excuse
10) a girl's dreams

Thinking question
What factors do you think would influence a speaker/writer to choose between the *of* relationship between nouns and the '-'s' relationship between nouns?

ACTIVITY 2.42

What grammatical or semantic features does the *italicized* item in each sentence have? Are there any categories that you can see (for example, *noun + noun*)?

1) It was a *no-win situation*.
2) The *oil tanker* turned over and sank.
3) The result was a *close-run thing*.
4) She was embroiled in a *family affair*.
5) Do you remember *'bicycle repair man'*?
6) Have you seen my *spectacle case*?
7) I left some money in my *jeans pocket*, and it got washed.
8) Kenya excels at *middle distance running*.
9) I'd forgotten my *identification tag* and had to avoid the *stadium security patrols*.
10) Yet again, he's hoping for *Cup glory*.

Thinking questions

What rules and generalizations about the relationships between nouns can you make as a result of this activity? List these.

Under what circumstances do you think hyphenated nouns such as 'breakfast-time' are created?

Further ideas

New things, new names

The late twentieth century is a period characterized by a rapid growth in the applications of technology to so many aspects of life. New machines are being created every year – these machines have to be named. Naming things is a powerful human need; we need to name phenomena and objects in the world in order to cope with complexity, and also to 'own' them in emotional terms. Identification is thus a central psychological concept. A feature of the naming process for the novelties of the late twentieth century is the complexity of the result in language. Parts in a motor car provide interesting examples:

- air cleaner retaining bolts
- fuel injection delivery system
- throttle valve stop earth cable
- crankcase ventilation system

To the uninitiated, these terms are a mystery. They can even be a barrier to coming to understand how a motor car works. What each complex phrase contains is a package of information which needs unpacking. As well as specifying objects, the phrases may also specify actions, their functions and relationships between the components. The English speaker listens or reads for the head word in a noun phrase – the head word dictates the agreement rules with the verbs, and is also the essence, either in reality or conceptually, of the object/phenomenon. What is the head word in the phrase 'throttle valve stop earth cable'? Is it 'cable'? If so, what is the relationship between the elements 'throttle valve stop earth' and the head word? No wonder uninformed people shake their heads when those in the know discuss familiar objects in terms which are incomprehensible. We have to know that the 'throttle valve stop' is electrically operated. So it needs an 'earth cable', not just any cable. The 'stop' is part of the throttle valve. The 'throttle valve' is one of many valves in any engine. Its type needs specifying. It is the one which controls the throttle. Examine the literature on computers or financial management or any other apparently arcane subject. Part of its complexity for the lay person is the complexity of the grammar of its components and activities.

Product words

The twentieth century is also characterized by advertising and the importance of brand names. Many product brand names have become the generic or class name for that particular product. The classic example is 'hoover', named after the company which was the market leader in the early days of vacuum cleaner production. Now we have a host of products which are synonymous with the objects. Like 'hoover', they have also become verbs as well as nouns. Here is a brief list: can you add to it?

xerox; tampax; tippex; walkman; pritt; polyfilla

Compile your own list of brand names in widespread use.

Initials as nouns

This work is being prepared on a PC. A CD is playing in the background. The work will be published in the UK. So many of the objects in our world are referred to by their initials. Organizations like the UN or IMF, or everyday objects like TV, are commonplace in speech and writing. We pronounce them 'you-kay' or 'tee-vee'. Some have become acronyms, where the letters become a word, like UNESCO or GATT. Newspapers and other media have had a strong influence on the dissemination of these terms and their now very widespread use. The initials are somehow more 'direct' than the full wording. The initials convey a real identity to the object or organization. A grammatical problem is whether the initial nouns are singular or plural. Notice the way they are used. Again, make a collection.

Headlines

A final influence on the use of noun phrases in the modern world is the newspaper headline. Some examples will help to explain this phenomenon:

- England on the rampage
- Shop hours reform at risk
- Troops in new coup attempt
- Income tax disappointment

None of these headlines contain verbs, at least on first examination. The verb is implied. Prepositions give a sense of movement or direction. The compact noun phrase that is the result has started to become a form of speech in itself on television news, which can often begin with 'headlines' of this type. Grammatical words like articles are omitted. The information is again packed in tightly, often ambiguously. This use of English has had an influence on the ways in which we tend to structure information in new compound nouns and noun phrases. A final example from a recent advertisement for a job:

FRONT OFFICE SYSTEMS DEVELOPERS

To deliver durable, object-oriented solutions for a demanding
derivatives trading environment

Can you work out what this means?

TASKS

A)   Read through the text which follows and then answer the questions.

Fast cars top in death crash figures

Angella Johnson

High performance cars are nearly twice as likely to be involved in fatal accidents than standard models, according to a Department of Transport report [5] published yesterday.

A breakdown of all accidents for 1990 showed the BMW 3 series, Volkswagen Golf GTi, Astra GTE and Ford Escort XR3i among cars [10] more likely to be in serious crashes.

Models registered before 1988 were the worst with 63 fatal or serious accidents per 10,000 vehicles. Newer cars appeared to have lower rates of injury [15] crashes, but the risk for company vehicles is increased by 30 per cent.

The report backed insurance companies which are planning measures to stop inexperienced drivers get-[20] ting behind the wheel of powerful machines.

The Association of British Insurers said premiums for fast cars had soared because of the greater likelihood they [25] would be in accidents, their attraction to thieves and high repair costs.

Fords are the most accident prone among the larger privately owned cars, with the Orion, Rover, Escort, [30] Sapphire and Granada heading the list. The company's latest RS Escort Cosworth has still to be given an insurance grouping but it has been suggested that a driver under 25 and [35] living in London might have to pay up to £12,000 a year for cover.

The modern small car less likely to be involved in a serious crash is the Volkswagen Polo – 105 per 10,000, [40] only 17 of which were serious or fatal. The most likely is the Fiat Uno at 153 per 10,000 – the average being 123.

The Mazda 323 is the 'safest' in the small/medium category and Volvos [45] best pick of the large cars (*Guardian*, 13 May 1992).

---

1)   Line   1: 'high performance cars' – what is the headword? Is this phrase used with the same frequency as 'saloon cars'?

2)   Line 8: 'Volkswagen Golf GTi'– what is the headword? Examine the other car names for the pattern of naming – what is it?

3)   Lines 4 and 22: What is the headword in each case, 'Department of Transport' and 'Association of British Insurers'? Is this a consistent pattern? (Make up or find other examples.)

4)   Line   3: *models;* line 14: *rates;* line 18: measures; line 23: premiums; line 26: costs. What are the common grammatical properties of these items?

5)   Line 36: 'cover' – are there similar items (grammatically) in the text? What are the grammatical features?

6) Line 37: 'Comment on the phrase 'modern small car' with reference to the order of adjectives.

B)   Collect noun compounds from newspapers, radio, TV, etc. Classify them. Look out for new ones.

Articles – definite and indefinite

Aim   To investigate the properties and functions of articles.

ACTIVITY 2.43

1)   Study the text which follows and note all instances of article usage – definite and indefinite (*a(n)* and *the*). Try to classify them according to their functions and meanings as you find them in the text. In order to do this, note the types of noun they precede, or noun phrase of which they form a part.
2)   Write working definitions of the articles on the basis of your previous knowledge and what you have found in the text.
3)   What advice about the meaning and use of articles in English would you want to pass on to a learner of English?
4)   Find the appropriate sections on articles and article usage in your reference grammar, and compare what you have found in your examination of the text and what is in the reference grammar. Note significant similarities and differences.

Several of the shops had gone out of business – they had been raided too often. The handful that had survived were screened behind folding metal shutters, drawn open just enough to allow access. An atmosphere of siege pervaded the precinct. A cold wind blew across the treeless undulations that passed for landscaping. Sheets of corrugated iron (Kirkby is rich in the stuff) and a mattress had been discarded in the dank 'adventure' playground. The more conventional type of playground was represented by a slide perched on a muddy mound. Drifts of waste paper and tins and bottles were washed up against walls.

What did it all mean? The wife of the motor-car worker would talk about 'common' people; the waitress would say it was how Kirkby liked to be; a nice middle-class lady blamed democracy; trade-unionists would blame unemployment; sociologists would talk about high-rise living and the break-up of communities. Society was running out of explanations. None of the explanations fitted; none could account for the rampant darkness of mind to which the devastations I had seen bore such eloquent witness. Those who worshipped punk rock worshipped that darkness. It signalled intellectual bankruptcy.

The man I spoke to at the Labour Club in Kirkby was gloomy. A whole generation was growing up without 'work experience'. There was hardly an eighteen-year-old in Kirkby who was in work. Given time, they would be not only unemployed but unemployable. Kirkby would not be released from its problems in the immediate future. New investment was in the offing. But new investment often meant new technology; new technology meant even fewer jobs. Machines were making men redundant. Nothing could be done about that. Progress was unstoppable. What was the solution? Earlier retirement? That would bring all the problems of leisure with it. Kirkby's problems were the problems of all industrial civilisation (Naipaul S., 1985: 246).

ACTIVITY 2.44

A)   Examine the sentences below. Each contains a possible error (or errors) in *article usage* made by learners of English:

- Can you correct each sentence? Decide what rule or principle the learner could be getting wrong in each case.
- Can you think of any circumstances under which each of the sentences could be correct?

1)   *White rhino is almost extinct.
2)   *She went up North on bus.
3)   *There were many expeditions to South Pole at turn of century.
4)   *I phoned up man I interviewed yesterday.
5)   *Margaret bought new dress and shoes.
6)   *The language is a complex phenomenon.
7)   *I went to the bed at 10 o'clock.
8)   *He lives on the Alma Road.
9)   *The eighteenth-century London was violent place.
10) *One of best stories I have read is the *David Copperfield*.
11) *You reach market through the narrow alley.
12) *She stayed for the lunch.
13) *It was the face-to-face confrontation.
14) *He spent large proportion of his life at the sea as a cook.
15) *The thieves approached at the nightfall.
16) *One of the most problematical aspects of the English is definite article.

B)   Distinguish between the meanings of the *italicized* items in the following pairs of sentences:

1) A.   Children play in *the forest* every day.
    B.   In some parts of the world, *the forest* is very important.

2) A.   I'd like *a large breakfast*.
   B.   I'd like *the large breakfast*.
3) A.   Many countries rely on *oil*.
   B.   Many countries rely on *the oil*.
4) A.   I've just received *a letter*.
   B.   I've just received *the letter*.

Thinking question

Do you think, on the basis of what you have found out in Activity 2.44, that the article in English poses a grammatical or a conceptual problem for investigators? Comment.

ACTIVITY 2.45

A)   English language teachers have long wished that there was a rule of thumb for article usage in English. Look at the ones teachers have tried to see if they work. Work out your own examples to show the effectiveness (or noneffectiveness) of the 'rules':

1) When you come across a noun, ask the question 'what particular one?' or 'which one?' If there's an answer put *the* before the noun. If not, use *a* or *an*.
2)   We always put the definite article before a noun if we know what it is we are talking about.
3) The indefinite article *a(n)* is used when the reference is vague.
4) Abstract nouns are not normally preceded by the definite article.
5) Mass nouns do not normally take the definite article. They behave rather like abstract nouns in this respect.
6) Names of countries do not take an article unless they precede a complex noun phrase like 'the United States', but for areas of water and land with accepted limits, the definite article is always used.

B)   Produce some 'rules' of your own – feel free to adapt the above.
C)   Comment on the value of these types of rule for 1) teachers and 2) learners.

Thinking questions

1) Do you think that giving learners examples of article usage in sentences is a good way of helping them understand the principles behind article usage?
2) Is there any advantage to be gained by providing samples of text for analysis and discussion of specific language points such as the article?

ACTIVITY 2.46

Refer to the texts in Activity 2.18 ('Common complaints') and Activity 2.42 ('Fast cars'), and answer the questions below.

Common complaints
1) Why no article with 'jet lag'? What would the use of *the* or *a* imply in this phrase?
2) Line 7: why '*the* travel agent'? What does this tell us about the author's understanding of the travel agent's role? See also '*the* holiday traveller' — line 13. Are there any other similar instances of this usage in the text?
3) What would be the effect if the author had decided to use *the* instead of *a* in the following phrases: line 6: 'a hazy idea'; lines 20–21: 'a slow business'; line 46: 'a trip'; line 72: 'a brain hormone'.

Fast cars
1) Look at the headline: would you include any articles if you were to write it out as a full sentence?
2) Lines 7–8: why 'the BMW' but not 'the Volkswagen'?
3) Lines 38–39: why 'the Volkswagen'?
4) What would be the meaning if 'the' was inserted in line 14: 'lower rates of injury'?
5) Line 34: why not say '*the* driver' instead of '*a* driver'?

Further ideas

Shared knowledge
The article *the* is used when the reader is assumed to have a shared knowledge of a topic with the writer. (The same would apply to listener and speaker.) If, for example, I say 'The university term hasn't yet begun', I am assuming that the listener knows which university I am talking about, or which university term. Similarly 'the match' in 'Did you see the match?' assumes that the listener shares my concept of 'the match'. When we are not aware of the context, or specific features of the context, such as when we have been away and encounter news headlines, or when we are in a foreign environment, there is potential for ambiguity. The problem for the second language speaker of English may be further compounded by the lack of this type of reference system in the person's native language.

Emphatic 'the'
'You don't mean *the* Mr Jones, do you?' One way in which we can and do play with the rules of article usage is to emphasize the article with, for example, a proper noun or name. It is very misleading therefore to refer to the article as

/ði:/. If it is referred to as /ðə/ there is less chance there will be a misunder-standing. The emphatic device is also used in advertising – 'IT'S *the* CAR TO BUY!' Such emphasis singles out the object from its field and makes it 'unique' in some way.

Be on the lookout for both of these features of article usage.

Becoming generic

'The police', 'the medical profession', 'the clergy' are all generic terms – groupings of people with common interests. If we talk of 'the environment', we are talking about the environment that is of relevance for all of us. The use of '*the*' with 'the police' has a different meaning. 'The police' are a collective or group sharing things in common, composed of individual police personnel, in much the same way as 'the management'. While we do not know the numbers of people concerned, we do know they share something in common. Can you think of any other terms like 'the police' which have emerged as generic or collective entities in the last few years, and which are always preceded by *the*?

Describing things

Aim   To examine some of the ways of describing things in English.

ACTIVITY 2.47

What do the *italicized* elements of the sentences which follow have in common? Can you put them into different categories according to their grammatical behaviour in these sentences?

1) They sailed to sea in a *beautiful pea-green* boat.
2) Johnson, who was beginning to tire, summoned up *one final effort*.
3) It's got a *fun fruity* flavour.
4) People *who live near the equator* are *more used* to the heat.
5) I've never known such *a wonderful group*!
6) I think your work is *rather good*.
7) It'll never be *the same*.
8) You're a *stronger* man than I am.
9) They have a *very well-drilled* squad of professionals.
10) She looked *mortified* when she heard the news.
11) He is *destined* for *great* things.
12) It was the *perfect* finish.
13) She is *lucky to be here*.

14) I often consult my *car maintenance* manual.
15) The rain *that fell* was *scarcely enough to fill the reservoirs*.

Thinking question
Do adjectives always describe nouns? Make up some examples to help.

ACTIVITY 2.48

Can you explain the following problems in English?

1) Why 'You can't be that bad' could be appropriate . . .
2) Why 'a blue old rusting car' might be incorrect . . .
3) Why 'It was a one-in-a-million chance' is correct usage . . .
4) Why there is a difference in meaning between 'safe journey' and 'journey-safe' . . .
5) An adjective like 'posh' can become 'posher', but an adjective like 'effective' becomes 'more effective' . . .
6) Why 'He is more of a man than you' and 'It's less a tree than a bush' are correct . . .

Thinking question
What specific types of knowledge (e.g., knowledge of the world, etc.) enable us to explain instances of the use of language as exemplified in this activity?

ACTIVITY 2.49

Below you will find a list of 'intensifiers'. Grade them from (1) most positive to most negative and (2) most extreme to least extreme.

> mildly   really   astonishingly   gratefully   deeply   seriously
> highly   somewhat   roughly   greatly   disturbingly   perfectly
> faintly   awfully   deliciously   surprisingly   absolutely
> totally   quite   notably   devastatingly   impeccably
> magnificently   appallingly

Thinking question
Are there restrictions as to the *type* of word (e.g. noun, adjective, etc.) which

can follow the intensifiers listed above? Make up your own examples in order to test any hypotheses you may have developed.

ACTIVITY 2.50

Divide the sentences which follow into two groups according to the function of the *italicized* parts.

1) My brother's an *early* riser.
2) You should aim *high* if you can.
3) The government got it badly *wrong*.
4) The castle was destroyed by a *direct* hit.
5) He complained that the problem was very *hard*.
6) She's sitting *pretty*.
7) It's a *long* and dusty road.
8) He plays it *long* into the penalty area.
9) They're very *close*.
10) She kept *still* and wasn't captured.

Thinking questions
Are there rules governing the use of adverbials like 'still' in the activity above? Can you state any rules on the basis of these sentences?

Further ideas

'Over the top'
'It's incredibly fantastically amazing', screams the sports commentator. The event being described is not exciting unless the commentator has responded in kind, verbally. English like other languages seems to be flexible and tolerant as a system in the way in which it absorbs the necessity of the broadcasting media to embellish events. Words that used to describe events and people are now used to emphasize the importance and impact of these events on the viewer. The commentary is intense – look at the 'intensifier' exercise (Activity 2.49) for further guidance and commentary, and the vocabulary from which the commentator draws. (If you know another language well, ask yourself whether or not the other language 'intensifies' in the same way in the media).

An analysis of the popular press reveals that adjectives to describe people and events (positively or negatively, but rarely neutrally) are very common. Adjectives like 'amazing', 'fabulous', 'rubbishy' and 'boring' are very common. Adjectives, as well as identifying properties and attributes of events, people and objects, also carry subjective meaning [see the following tasks].

As well as a trend towards overstatement or hyperbole, there is also a trend in British English usage towards understatement or pathos. An ecstatically happy person is 'quite thrilled' to discover they have won the National Lottery. We affect listeners and readers with our use of adjectives or their equivalents.

Advertising

Advertising copy stretches language. This advertising language finds its way into our daily vocabulary without our noticing it. We perhaps do not realize that we start talking about a 'fun way of having a holiday'. Fun has only recently moved into a premodifying position in noun phrases, equivalent to an adjective. It might be interesting to decide whether 'fun' is an adjective –can we say 'The most fun holiday we've ever had'? or 'A really fun afternoon'? 'This holiday is fun'?. The need for snappy slogans and bending of language has introduced us to new and creative ways of exploiting the grammar of English. What this has shown is that the grammar and the lexicon of the language are so closely enmeshed that to talk of grammar and vocabulary as if they were separate is to distort reality. If we want a word to be a verb, we can make it a verb. So it can't be too much of a step to begin talking of 'funning' as in 'My friend was funning himself in Florida'. Old hands might object to the stretching and bending of their 'beautiful' language. But language is infinitely flexible and creative. If poets can stretch language, why not copy writers? People need to be able to express their own thoughts. Perhaps the explosion of the noun phrase and the adjective is the first phase of the emergence of a plurality of dialects? After all, isn't 'sociospeak' (as it is known – writing on sociology) really a profusion of nouns and adjectives, an attempt to encapsulate complex ideas in economical fashion? For instance, 'The political form of the liberationist understanding of sociology . . .' (Berger and Kellner, 1981: 113).

For the time being we will eat our 'big big breakfast cereal' and think about 'sunning ourselves' in hot countries. The writers of advertising copy will continue to be creative. On the one hand, we may know more, see more, realize more, and need to adapt the language to express what we see and know. On the other hand, advertising copy writers may have different plans in mind – they may want to influence our perceptions of what we see and know.

Note In grammar practice books, and in reference grammars, there is little information on the ways in which the noun phrase has developed and changed, and ways of describing things. Perhaps this is an area in which the individual investigator can come up with more insights from the perspectives? Keep your eyes and ears open!

TASKS

A)   Refer to the texts in Activity 2.13 ('Fishermen survive six months adrift') and Activity 2.43 (from Naipaul, 1985) and answer the questions which follow.

Fishermen survive six months adrift
1) Find the following words in the text: *starving* (line 1) *recorded* (line 7) and *upturned* (line 10). What word class do they fall into? What is their function in the text?
2) Line 27: what sort of word is 'outboard' in 'outboard motor'?
3) Find the following phrases:
   line 14 − '*South* Pacific'; line 16 − '*Western* Samoa'; line 18 − '*eastern* end'; and line 32 − '*southeast* of'. What is the function of the italicized word in each case? What do you learn about geographical directions and compass locations? Are the terms 'south' and 'southern' interchangeable, for example?

Naipaul
1) Line 2: in the phrase 'folding metal shutters', what actually folds?
2) Line 5: do you know of any other substance or object that is 'corrugated', or is 'corrugated iron' an item in its own right?
3) Line 6: 'dank "adventure" playground' − why is 'adventure' in parenthesis? Is 'adventure' an adjective? Similarly, is 'intellectual' in 'intellectual bankruptcy' (line 17) an adjective?
4) Line 25: is 'unstoppable' an adjective? If so, what does it describe? Can you find any other sentence formed in the same way in this text?

B)   Record instances of *intensifier* use that are new to you. Survey the newspapers, television and radio for up-to-the-minute expressions.

C)   *Looking for adjective use in the press*. Collect, over a period of say, one week, examples of adjective use in newspaper reports in the tabloids and broadsheets. Which type of newspaper, and in which types of report are adjectives used most frequently in the 'subjective', or opinionated, sense?

D)   Make a collection of advertising slogans in which nouns are used as adjectives or in adjective position (premodifying or as complements).

Comparing things

Aim   To examine various ways of expressing comparison in English.

Pretask

List as many ways as possible in which you can compare things, people, events, etc., in English which do not use the '*adjective* + *er* (or variant) . . . *than*' form ('bigger than').

ACTIVITY 2.51

Look at the sentences which follow. They all compare things. Complete a table like the one below, showing what is compared with what, and what the basis of the comparison is.

1)   I like the smaller design myself.
2)   The temperature was higher than it had been for months.
3)   He became lighter as the diet worked.
4)   I'd have cooked something more spicy if I'd known you were coming.
5)   The work has been more professionally finished this year.
6)   She was writing a book longer than *War and Peace*.
7)   I was less concerned about the result than my colleagues.
8)   We should be more responsive to our students' needs.
9)   If you don't like this book, there's a better one coming out soon.
10)   She was faster about the court than her opponent.

	Element 1	Element 2	Basis of comparison
1			
2			
3			
4			
5			
6			
7			
8			
9			
10			

Thinking question

Write out a series of simple rules for comparing things in English on the basis of this activity.

ACTIVITY 2.52

Can you explain the differences in meaning between the pairs of sentences which follow?

1)　A.　It was so difficult a problem that I gave up trying to solve it.
　　B.　It was such a difficult problem that I gave up trying to solve it.
2)　A.　It was too good to eat.
　　B.　It was good enough to eat.
3)　A.　One foot was shorter than the other, which was a problem.
　　B.　The shorter of the two feet was the problem.
4)　A.　This idea was the most exciting.
　　B.　This was a most exciting idea.
5)　A.　The position she adopted was less than reasonable.
　　B.　The position she adopted was less reasonable than I had expected.
6)　A.　I don't think I could have done a better job myself.
　　B.　I don't think I could have done the job better myself.
7)　A.　The window was as high up the wall as a coconut palm.
　　B.　The window was the height of a coconut palm up the wall.
8)　A.　It's not as difficult as you thought.
　　B.　It's less difficult than you think.
9)　A.　Of all the teachers I have known, she is the most inspiring.
　　B.　She is the most inspiring teacher I have known.
10)　A.　As you enter the city, so the amount of litter increases.
　　B.　The further into the city you go, the more litter there is.

Thinking question
How much does a speaker/writer's opinion seem to influence the choice of comparative structure which they use? (Refer to the above examples.)

ACTIVITY 2.53

Into what different categories would you place the comparative sentences which follow? What are the defining characteristics of each category?

1)　We'll pay by the length or by the weight, whichever is the most appropriate.
2)　It was the biggest of his punches.
3)　He smokes like a chimney.
4)　The harder they come the harder they fall.
5)　James was the taller of the twins.
6)　It felt like Christmas.

7) Not so much a game, more a way of life.
8) She was rather economical with the truth.
9) It was quite the most breathtaking view you can imagine.
10) Any more of that nonsense and you'll be kicked out.

Thinking question
What do you learn about English usage from the attempt to create categories of different types of comparative structure?

Further ideas

Fact and opinion
The comparative structure enables a speaker/writer to express a specific opinion or point of view about a subject. It could be claimed that the use of various intensifiers is, in itself, an indication of the writer's point of view, and in a sense is comparative. Intensifiers only have relative or comparative meaning. Fact is likely to be expressed in the least flamboyant language; opinion is likely to be encoded in intensified and superlative language. For example,

My brother is taller than me (fact).
My brother is incredibly tall (opinion).

Absolute or relative?
Are there any absolute factual comparisons in our world or is the language we use a way of indicating, in very subjective ways, that we *believe* one thing to be better than another? And in our lives, it might turn out to be the *best*. It is our way of being individual, of expressing our own individual perceptions about the world. We may tend to exaggerate, but we seem to need to stamp what we see and experience with our own very individual judgements, which are often expressed in the language of comparison.

TASKS

1) In the text in Activity 2.42 ('Fast cars') a number of things have been compared. List the things which have been compared and the ways in which they have been compared. Are there ways of comparing which have not been dealt with in the activities in this section?
2) Go through other texts in this book and find instances where comparison is made. Note all ways in which this is done, and then check against your reference grammar for confirmation. Are all instances that you have found catered for?

Pronouns — substituting

Aim   To explore various aspects of pronoun usage and meaning.

ACTIVITY 2.54

Identify the parts of each of the following utterances which replace a longer word or phrase. What is the *full meaning* in each case? For example, 'It's mine' means 'it(?) belongs to me'.

1)   That pen is hers.
2)   The big one belongs to me.
3)   It's in your hands — it's up to you.
4)   I did it myself.
5)   Which is yours?
6)   Nobody knows my name.
7)   This has no real meaning.
8)   He injured himself.
9)   We should all love one another.
10)   Where it fell I have no idea.

Thinking questions
Is it easy to understand the utterances above? Do you need contextual information in order to understand them?

ACTIVITY 2.55

As you read the text which follows answer the questions to which the numbered superscripts refer.

Festive lights leave shoppers in the dark

Plymouth's Christmas lights failed to shine for the start of the first of *this year's*[1] late night shopping days.

And the city council today said [5] they knew about the problem but *it*[2] appeared a contractor had been unable to shed any festive light on the proceedings until later in the evening.

Today John Brady, manager of the [10] Armada Centre, said shoppers were put off coming up the hill towards North Cross roundabout because *the street*[3] was so dark.

A council spokesman said *they*[4] were [15] aware that the lights were not on at 4.30 and told the contractor responsible who said he turned the lights back on at 6 pm.

'Apparently there is a problem with [20] the time clocks and *he*[5] is looking into it, *he*[6] said.

The city engineers are to look at the situation tonight to try to sort it out for next Thursday.

[25] But the evening was still a success according to Steve Golding, chairman of the late night shopping committee.

'One of the major department stores said *they*[7] had a 33 per cent increase on [30] their figure last year,' he said.

'Looking good'

The whole atmosphere of the run-up to Christmas boded well for the traders, 90 per cent of which were open late [35] into the evening, he added.

'With just under four weeks to go before Christmas, *things*[8] are looking good' (*Plymouth Evening Herald*, 27 November 1992).

Questions

1) Is there another way of expressing 'this year'?
2) What does 'it' mean in this sentence?
3) Which 'street'?
4) What are 'they'?
5) Who is 'he'?
6) Is this the same 'he' as in the quotation?
7) How can a department store be 'they'?
8) What is meant by 'things'?

Thinking question

Cross-refer to your reference grammar on the topic of 'pronouns'. Do your findings in Activities 2.54 and 2.55 coincide with what the grammar says?

Clauses

Aim   To investigate the functions and meanings of clauses in sentences and in discourse.

ACTIVITY 2.56

What do all the *italicized* parts of the sentences – clauses – which follow have in common? Classify them into any groups you think are appropriate.

1) He was tired *because it was hot.*
2) *To tell you the truth* I'm not that happy.
3) It's not *as if she's so famous.*
4) Come and meet my new friend, *who's just back from a long sea voyage.*
5) Hydrochloric acid, *whether it's concentrated or not*, must be kept in a locked cupboard.
6) We just didn't expect *the shops would be shut.*
7) Drink this, *it'll give you a lift.*
8) It was pouring with rain *when I left.*
9) You'd better watch the fire *in case the baby goes too near it.*
10) Just drop in *whenever you're passing.*
11) We had our holidays in Brittany again, *where we went last year.*
12) He was there, *I said.*
13) *While I don't mind the expense*, I'm worried about the long delay.
14) *Carrying a long spear*, he entered the room.
15) She ran from the building, *too scared to speak.*
16) Heineken reaches the parts *other beers can't reach.*

ACTIVITY 2.57

The sentences in Activity 2.56 are divided into two parts (*italicized* and nonitalicized). Are the different parts of these sentences different in kind or meaning?

Try reversing the order of the parts of these sentences. What is the effect on (1) the grammar and (2) the meaning of the sentences of reversing those parts which can be reversed?

Are there any which are impossible to reverse? Why?

Thinking questions
What have you discovered about clauses in English as a result of these activities? What, for example, have you learned about meanings and functions of clauses?

Would you agree that some clause structures and sentence structures in English are more difficult to understand than others? Which of the 16 sentences in Activity 2.56 would you regard as most difficult? What are your criteria?

ACTIVITY 2.58

Answer the following questions on the text in Activity 2.15 ('Weather watch')

1) Lines 1–3: what element of meaning is provided by the clause beginning with 'When' and ending with 'Egypt'?
2) Lines 12–13: how many clauses in this sentence?
3) Lines 29–31: what is the meaning of the clause beginning with 'as'? Does it have the same meaning as the clause beginning 'as' in line 38? Or the clause beginning 'As' in line 43?
4) Do you notice anything about the way in which the writer has employed the clause system in English in this text?

Thinking questions

How far do you think it is true to say that the clause is a basic unit of meaning in English? Because any element which is smaller will simply not have enough connected information to express a full meaning? In other words, phrases and words only make sense within a clause structure. A focus on the verb, for example, may be misleading in terms of total meaning, unless it is the imperative form – 'Help!'

Go through the same text ('Weather watch'), sentence by sentence. Complete a table like the one shown below, according to the way the information is presented in the text – that is, whether the information is central (*main*), or *subordinate* in terms of its meaning in the text.

Main	Subordinate

ACTIVITY 2.59

A)   Comment on the functions of the parts of the sentences which are *italicized* in the examples below:

1)   *The man we need* is Wilson.
2)   *Whoever did that* should be shot.
3)   Mary, *who's having a baby next year*, has given up smoking.
4)   That's the car *that I want*.
5)   Do you know the place *where I work*?
6)   It's not *something that she'd like to be remembered for*.
7)   You were the only person *I could turn to*.
8)   *Whatever the next step* we should be very careful.
9)   He was *a beaten man*.
10) The things *we used to do* just aren't fashionable any more.

B)   Comment on the meanings of the *italicized* parts of the following sentences. Are there different types of relationship grammatically and in terms of meaning with the other part of each sentence? List some of the differences.

1)   The goal *I scored* will be long remembered.
2)   Someone *who has lots of money* can buy that car.
3)   When she saw the amount *I was eating* she nearly fainted.
4)   I don't like dog owners *who cannot keep their animals under control*.
5)   *The man I hit* was trying to hit me.
6)   Everyone *who runs hard* has a chance of a gold medal.
7)   I have a lot of time for people *who try*.
8)   Whatever *you try to do* has potential.
9)   The plans *we made* were quickly abandoned.
10) She realized that this was someone *who was going to challenge her*.

Thinking question
How far do you agree with the idea that the more clauses there are in a text, and the more subtle their relationships, the more difficult the text is to process for a reader?

ACTIVITY 2.60

What explanations would you give for the following occurrences?

1)   The use of commas in the sentence: 'Malcolm, who was very fond of spending money, was fired by his employers'.

2) Why some speakers might regard the following sentence as incorrect: 'These are the people I'm indebted to.'
3) Why a non-native speaker might produce a sentence like the following: *'The garden which it is beautiful can be visited at any time.'
4) Why a sentence like the following might cause problems in understanding: 'She lived in a newly painted house near the road to Barnchester, a small town of 200 inhabitants.'
5) The difference between: 'It is a comfortable chair' and 'It is a chair which is comfortable.'
6) The differences in meaning between:

I know a man. He has many friends.
I know a man who has many friends.
I know a man, who has many friends.
I know a man with many friends.
I know a friendly man.
A man I know has many friends.

ACTIVITY 2.61

With reference to the text in Activity 2.18 ('Common complaints'), answer the questions which follow:

1) Can you rewrite the sentence which covers lines 4–7 in order to make the relative relationship explicit? Use 'who' to mark the relative clause.
2) What is the more important information in the sentence in lines 12–15, and how are you able to tell?
3) What two elements of the sentence in lines 16–19 are linked by the relative 'which'? Are there any other sentences in the text which feature the same type of relative structure?
4) Look at the sentence which begins on line 44. How many relative clauses are in this sentence, and what is their function?
5) Who is the text written about? List the references to people in the text, specific and not so specific. Which ones need a relative clause to specify their identity or characteristics?

Thinking questions
Check your reference grammar for information on relative clauses. How much of what you have found out in these activities is confirmed by the grammar? Is there any topic not covered? If so, where might you find assistance? Have you learned anything new about clauses from these exercises?

Further ideas

Grammaticization

Rutherford (1987) has advanced the notion that as a learner of a language gains in proficiency, the learner's command of clause structure becomes increasingly sophisticated. This is part of the process he calls 'grammaticization'. The process can, of course, work in the opposite direction, where we try to be more direct by using fewer subordinate clauses in our speech and writing. Indeed, some public figures have been criticized for using too many clauses, of being 'unnecessarily verbose' in their speech. Too many subordinate clauses might give the impression of too many exceptions or qualifications to a position and therefore they undermine its credibility. A range of complex clauses is all very well in written text where such conventions are often accorded a high value. In spoken text it seems we prefer the speaker who comes to the point, who makes direct statements. *What do you think?*

TASKS

Look through an academic textbook. Select a page of complete text. Note the average sentence length in terms of number of clauses. What does your reaction to the text tell you about

1) your own preference for writing styles;
2) the writer's way of using language; and
3) the relationship between clarity of explanation by the writer and your under-standing of the topic?

Look at the following example, and also at the extracts on p. 14 from Halliday, Gumperz and Lyons. What is your view regarding sentence length, textual complexity and readability?

> If one defines intellectuals as members of a profession in any narrow sense, their identification in pre-literate societies would be difficult, though not perhaps impossible. Certainly there were no scholars of Chou Chin's kind. If we define the term in a larger sense, of individuals engaged in the creative exploration of culture [. . .] then I would argue that this type of activity is more clearly present, even in the 'simpler' societies. As a result of certain tendencies in the social sciences, the presence of this kind of activity, this kind of individual, has been obscured. The contribution of the intellect in simple societies has been played down to such an extent that one is sometimes moved to ask 'Do natives think?'. Or do they just have constraining structures, special systems of classification, undomesticated thought? (Goody, 1977: 20).

Time and clause structure

Aim   To investigate the ways in which different sentence and clause types deal with the question of time.

ACTIVITY 2.62

A) Identify the finite verbs in the sentences which follow (the rough rule of thumb is one finite verb per clause – try this to see if it works).
B) Divide the sentences into *clauses* – main and subordinate.
C) Decide on the time relationships between the clauses in each sentence – for example, are the time relationships sequential or simultaneous?

1) It was a beautiful morning and the sun was pouring in through the windows.
2) It rained when I was waiting for the bus.
3) The people were leaving the dance while I was walking home.
4) While I ate, the children were playing.
5) Because I was feeling ill, I stayed at home.
6) He recognized me, although I had changed a lot.
7) She said she had had enough to eat, so I had to go.
8) If he had received any mail, he would jump for joy.
9) The musician played while the shoppers shuffled past.
10) If I had the chance, I'd take it with open arms.

ACTIVITY 2.63

1)   List the subordinate clause markers in the sentences in Activity 2.62. Look at the subordinate clause marker in each of the sentences and decide whether it is a *time* marker or indicator. If it is a time marker/indicator, remove it from the sentence in order to see the effect on the meaning and grammar of the sentence; note the effect in each case. Is there any change in the relationship between the events in the two clauses as a result of this operation? Can the sentences be 'repaired' without putting the time marker back? For example, 'I looked up when you came into the room.' Remove 'when' – *'I looked up you came into the room.' Two separate sentences are required: 'I looked up. You came into the room.' The relationship between the sentences is now ambiguous – the reader must make the connection in time.
2)   What is the effect of (1) changing the order of the clauses in each sentence;

and (2) moving the time marker to the beginning of the main clause? Does it change the time relationship? For example,

'I looked up when you came into the room.'
When you came into the room I looked up.
When I looked up you came into the room.

Thinking questions
What types of choice does a speaker/writer have available in structuring sentences? What is the nature of this choice? What is the connection between these choices and meanings that the speaker/writer wishes to convey?

ACTIVITY 2.64

Read through the following text and answer the questions below it.

Heatwave prompts cover-up alert as skin cancer risk rises

Madeleine Bunting

Doctors yesterday issued warnings to cover up *as temperatures reached the 20s(C) 70s(F)*.

Skin cancer has doubled every 10 years since the 1930s and screening cream and small doses of sun are being advised by the Imperial Cancer Research Fund, especially for fair-skinned, freckly people.

At one point earlier this year the ozone layer, which provides protection against cancer-causing ultra-violet radiation, had dwindled by up to 20 per cent over northern Europe. One amateur's calculation is that for every 1 per cent drop in the ozone layer's thickness, there could be a 2 per cent increase in non-melanoma skin cancers. However, the National Radiological Protection Board said yesterday that readings were no higher than average.

Britain's coldest village turned into a suntrap, recording 27°C (81°F) according to amateur readings. Braemar, in the Scottish Highlands, has twice held the national low-temperature record with −27.2°C.

The Aberdeen weather centre reported a highest temperature of 20°C (68°F) in Kinloss at the end of the worst season in 30 years for Scotland's ski resorts.

With temperatures likely to hit the mid-20sC (mid-70sF) in London today, animals were being doused with hosepipes to cool off at an Asda festival of food and farming in Hyde Park, London (*Guardian*, 14 May 1992).

1) Lines 2–3: does the italicized clause have a time reference?
2) Identify all time references in the sentence beginning 'Skin' (line 4) and ending 'people' (line 9).
3) When had the ozone layer dwindled by up to 20 per cent?
4) Is it clear when Braemar recorded a temperature of 27.2°C?
5) Why is there an apparent contradiction in time reference in lines 34–39?
6) List all *point in time* references in the text. List all *specific time* references in the text. Do you notice any lack of accuracy with regard to time references in the text? Is there any ambiguity regarding time reference?

Thinking questions

1) How far do you agree with the idea that verb tense only provides a fraction of information about time in any sample of language?
2) Refer back to Activities 2.56–2.58. Do relative clauses add any information about time? Is the classification of clauses based on subordinate clause markers helpful? (For example is 'when' only a marker for time clauses?)

Condition and concession

Aims To explore ways in which condition and concession add to text meaning.

ACTIVITY 2.65

Comment on the following statements.

1) There are three types of conditional sentence in English.
2) All conditional clauses begin with *if* or *unless* in the case of a negative condition.
3) Conditional sentences can refer to past, present and future time in English.

How far do you agree with each one? What evidence can you provide to support your views? Look up the topics of condition and concession in at least three reference grammars. What is the view of each of the grammars?

ACTIVITY 2.66

Identify and describe the type of condition that each of the following sentences exemplifies:

1) I'll lend you the money if you promise to repay it.

2)   I'll lend you the money so long as you don't waste it.
3)   I'll sell you my car provided that you don't crash it.
4)   I'll take my spare keys in case I lose the others.
5)   I'll sell you my car on condition that you don't resell it.
6)   I won't lend you any money unless you promise to repay it.
7)   Unless I've made a mistake, you're the man I met yesterday.
8)   If it's raining, you need an umbrella.
9)   They might run away if they saw your scars.
10) If he isn't praised, he'll never make the grade.

What shades of meaning are exemplified by the conditions in the sentences above, in terms of 'functions'? What do you think the speaker is trying to achieve in each case? For example, do any give advice?

Complete a table as follows.

	Condition	Function
1		
2		
3		
4		
5		
6		
7		
8		
9		
10		

ACTIVITY 2.67

Below you will find pairs of statements.

1)   Try connecting them with both *if* and *although*.
2)   Try inserting *if* and *although* at the beginning of the sentences and between the pairs.

Note the effects of the different conjunctions and the different positions of the conjunctions on the meaning of the sentences.

Example: He is mad. He is happy.

He is mad *if* he is happy.
He is mad *although* he is happy.

If he is mad, he is happy.
Although he is mad, he is happy.

1) She is successful. She is tight-fisted.
2) It's raining steadily. The roads won't be flooded.
3) The manual is quite difficult to read. The language is convoluted.
4) He went to bed early. He was worn out.
5) The law was strict. It was not unfair.
6) Many people enjoy cigarettes. It is an antisocial habit.
7) I don't enjoy opera. You must not expect me to listen.
8) The rains have begun. We shall begin planting the crops.

What conclusions do you draw about the notions of condition and concession from this exercise? What are the most striking differences? Where are the overlaps?

Thinking question
Would reversing the order of the clauses have any effect on the meaning of the sentences above?

ACTIVITY 2.68

1)   Answer the questions on the text which follows:

Hydrogen car that goes like a bomb

John Vidal talks to the visionary Mazda boss pioneering a vehicle that runs on water

In two or three years' time the first
[5] hydrogen-powered cars will be road-tested. In two or three decades, predicts Michinori Yamanouchi, managing director of Mazda, his company will be making hundreds of thousands
[10] of the pollution-free cars each year. By the second half of the 21st century, he suggests, hydrogen will be the most popular fuel in the world for industry.

It's a vision to inspire some future
[15] hope. 'Today, the issue facing all mankind is environmental preservation. The greatest challenge to the world car industry is to reduce carbon dioxide emissions,' he says, confident
[20] that technology will reduce exhaust emissions to almost nothing within a decade or so.

Hydrogen is the fuel of the future he says: no carbon dioxide emissions,
[25] great spin-offs to industry and power generators, no danger, all but free, limitless fuel from water or many other sources, and the one real alternative to the fossil fuel economy.
[30] If the vision seems similar to those of the nuclear pioneers, Yamanouchi is not worried. It is, he says, the only way for the car industry – indeed, the world – to go in environmentally sensitive
[35] post-Rio times.

Mazda, world leader along with Mercedes Benz in hydrogen-engine research, is so convinced of hydrogen's potential to take over the petrol
[40] economy that it is spending hundreds of millions of pounds in research and development over the next decade to be in the lead when the environment demands an end to transport as we
[45] know it.

The hydrogen engine is no longer a dream, he says. A Mazda prototype hydrogen car last year achieved 90 mph and travelled 125 miles. The main goals
[50] now are to reduce engine weight and increase the distances that can be travelled. Safety has been worked out; so too has the fuel, which can be extracted from water and on combustion returns
[55] to water. The 'tank', which is filled with a granulated metal hydride, can be shaped to any layout.

The real problem, says Yamanouchi, will be to set up an infrastructure of
[60] hydrogen stations to support the cars. Here he looks to governments committed to sustainable development for help.

Not that Yamanouchi believes
[65] things will be very different in future. The car, he agrees, will remain a toy of the rich, although he predicts a rise in car use of only 3 per cent in the developed world and a 10 per cent
[70] increase in cars used in the developing world in the next decade – well below the suggestions of the Department of Transport.

He accepts that the car in itself is not
[75] necessarily the most damaging player in the environment but the roads and development that are needed to service them.

'Where does the role of the car-
[80] maker end?' he asks. 'That is difficult. The automobile society must be based on sharing responsibilities equally between car-makers, governments and customers.'
[85] By initiating the research that potentially means the end of one fifth of the world's carbon emissions within 50 years, Yamanouchi may well be thought to have done his own particu-
[90] lar share (*Guardian*, 3 July 1992).

1) Michinori Yamanouchi is 'confident' (line 19). Are there any conditions to modify this confidence, as mentioned in the text?
2) What type of conditional is the clause in lines 30–32?
3) Yamanouchi believes that the car is a 'toy of the rich' (lines 66–67). Does he make any concessions?
4) Is there a *central* underlying condition to the success of the hydrogen-powered car? What evidence is there in the text?
5) Does Yamanouchi make any concessions (in the report) to petrol-engined cars?

Thinking questions

Compare the amount of conditionality in the text above with the texts in Activity 2.10 ('Bard . . .'), Activity 2.24 (*The Daily Telegraph* letter) and Activity 2.43 (Naipaul). What differences do you notice? Do any of the texts make concessions to the reader, or refer to concessions made by actors in the texts?

Cause, reason, purpose

Aims   To examine meanings of cause, reason and purpose in texts.

Pretask

Distinguish in your own words between *cause* and *reason* for the occurrence of an event. Do you see *purpose* or *result* having an overlap in meaning with cause and reason?

ACTIVITY 2.69

In each of the sentences which follow, identify the subject and then decide whether you think the subject is the *actor* – i.e., is directly responsible for the action – or the *means/instrument* – i.e., is the agent of the action, and not responsible as such.

1) Some children rang my doorbell and ran away.
2) The commandos blew up the ammunition dump.
3) The supplies were brought yesterday.
4) A single punch knocked him off his feet.
5) A lorry delivered copies of *The Times*.
6) They narrowed their focus.
7) Football started in the Middle Ages.

8)   Ossie opened the door.
9)   He grew in stature as the tournament progressed.
10) The talks collapsed without reason.

Now describe any differences in meaning between the following pairs of sentences.

1) A.   Her house is being painted.
    B.   She is having her house painted.
2) A.   The gang wounded him with a knife.
    B.   A knife wounded him.
3) A.   The post came early this morning.
    B.   They delivered the post early this morning.
4) A.   Do you type these exercises?
    B.   Do you have these exercises typed?

Thinking questions
What statements can you make regarding the meaning of the verb in each of the above examples? What can you say about the way *cause* and *effect* is dealt with in these examples? Check your ideas with at least two reference grammars. Are your ideas confirmed?

ACTIVITY 2.70

Examine the following set of sentences and classify them according to whether they describe *cause* or *reason*, or *result* or *purpose*. Underline the part of the sentence which has this function in each example:

1)   I gave her £40 because she said she needed it.
2)   His lateness lost him his job.
3)   The hot weather caused many illnesses.
4)   Now that we've sorted out that problem, we'll be able to get on with it.
5)   He was envious of his brother being chosen.
6)   She gave up her quest because of her age.
7)   To help catch the criminal they are putting the case on TV.
8)   He was commended for his gallantry.
9)   As I was the fastest runner, they sent me ahead.
10) Hard work leads to fatigue.
11) He cried because of the pain.
12) She ran quickly to catch the bus to College.
13) The area has an equable climate and consequently is very good for agriculture.
14) The pound fell because the economy was in a bad way.

15) He ran to hide out of a sense of shame.
16) The effect of too much work is to blunt the mind's sharpness.
17) Her success came from hours of careful preparation.
18) I didn't want to talk to them so I slammed the door in their face.
19) Grammar is complex. Therefore it needs careful analysis.
20) His outrageous behaviour made him a laughing stock.
21) The programme having finished, she retired to bed.
22) Deforestation often brings about soil erosion.

List as below the different ways of signalling reason, result, cause and purpose as you have found them in the above examples. Can you classify them in any way, for example, structural, lexical, etc?

Reason

Result

Cause

Purpose

Thinking question
Look back over your findings in this and the previous section. Do you see the meanings of such areas as condition and concession, cause and reason reflected only at sentence level, or do the meanings extend over whole texts?

ACTIVITY 2.71

Refer to the texts in Activity 2.64 ('Heatwave') and Activity 2.68 ('Hydrogen car'). Answer the questions which follow.

Heatwave
1) Identify a central cause in the text. What are the results?
2) Is 'screening cream' (lines 5–6) effect or result?
3) What is the result of a '1 per cent drop in the ozone layer's thickness (lines 16–17)?'
4) Why are animals being 'doused with hosepipes' (lines 36–37)? Purpose or reason?

Hydrogen car
1) What are the likely effects of switching to hydrogen engines? (lines 23–29). How are these signalled in the text?
2) What is the result of Mazda's conviction with regard to hydrogen engines? (lines 38–43). What is the grammatical structure?

3) How are the goals of Mazda's research expressed? (lines 49–52).
4) Of all the events and processes reported in the article, which is most central in terms of its effects? Draw a simple visual to represent this.

Further ideas

Central causes?

Any text which reports a series of events is likely to specify, either overtly or covertly, a main cause of these events. Similarly, it is likely that any text which contains a number of conditions will contain a central condition which subordinates the others. Cause and certain conditionals seem to be quite closely related as it turns out; the difference is that the condition is often only a theoretical cause: 'If you stay at home, you will be bored.' The cause of the boredom is staying at home – *if* the person actually stays.

While there could be a number of causes for a particular series of events, the writer will usually, through the structure and organization of the text, specify a particular cause as central, with all other events and processes resulting from this cause. The choice of particular sentence patterns from among the possible patterns will enable the writer to direct the reader's attention towards specific messages in the text. Thus there may well be stronger signals of cause and effect in certain structures than in others:

In order to catch the bus, she ran.
She ran for the bus.
She ran because she wanted to catch the bus.
She ran, as she had to catch the bus.

You may be able to detect the stronger message in these examples. 'Because' signals a weaker reason than 'to', which appears most purposeful. We are more certain with 'for the bus' – there seems to be little other reason or purpose in her running.

TASK

Go over the text in Activity 2.43 (Naipaul) – the author points out a number of problems. Does he specify causes? Or is his message more subtle? Are any conditions or concessions offered for what he sees?

Direct and indirect speech — who said what?

Aim To examine the conventions for reporting and quoting speakers in texts.

ACTIVITY 2.72

A) Make up a set of rules for reporting direct speech. In order to help, you can convert the examples of direct speech below into indirect speech, and make rules from the operations you have performed.

1) 'I want to go home,' John said.
2) 'You have nothing more to say,' they told him.
3) 'There are only three alternatives,' she said.
4) 'I think it's a good idea to wait,' he said.

B) Convert the following utterances into reported speech. Note any exceptions to the rules you have made in the task above.

1) 'He walks to work every day,' said Oliver.
2) 'They had eaten before I arrived,' she said.
3) 'You must wake up,' she said.
4) 'You should help old people,' said Jack.
5) 'The Sun is 93 million miles away,' said Rupert.
6) 'I enjoy playing handball,' said Diego.
7) 'Britain is recovering,' said Mrs Thatcher.
8) 'I once saw Harold Wilson,' said the old man.

Thinking question
In colloquial English speech, are any of the 'rules' for reporting speech that you have made up broken?

ACTIVITY 2.73

Convert the following questions (all asked by a person called Barry) into reported speech, noting any further rules for reporting speech as you do the task.

1) 'Why are you crying?'
2) 'When are you leaving?'
3) 'What's your name?'
4) 'Did Liverpool lose?'
5) 'Which window shall I open?'

6) 'Why won't you help me?'
7) 'Is this my pen or his?'
8) 'Should I go or should I stay?'

Thinking question

Do you notice any differences between the reporting of statements and questions?

ACTIVITY 2.74

Make a list of as many 'verbs of saying' as you can. Note the different types of reported clause which the different verbs take. For example, many verbs take a *that* clause ('I said *that* . . .). Some verbs take a *to* clause ('She asked me *to* be quiet').

What sorts of reported clause do the various 'verbs of saying' take? Can you create categories of the types of verbs of saying?

Are there any other aspects of reported structures that might cause difficulties? For example, the position of the object?

Now check your rules and categories against the relevant section in your reference grammar. Do you see any discrepancies between your ideas and those in the grammar?

ACTIVITY 2.75

What was said?

Turn these sentences into direct speech, by writing down the actual words that you think were said. For example,

She alleged that I had stolen her bicycle.
'You've stolen my bicycle.'

1) The weatherman forecasts snow tonight.
2) I was commanded to sit down.
3) She vowed to help me.
4) The doctor recommended that you try to give up smoking.
5) They requested that they should be allowed to go home.
6) I offered to assist.
7) She suggested that I had made a mistake.
8) He asserted that I was wrong.
9) He demanded that I return his clothes.
10) Conner swore to get the Cup back.

Thinking question
What are the implications of this activity for the ways in which we interpret what others say, and the ways in which we report these?

ACTIVITY 2.76

Refer to the texts listed below. In these texts, there is a mixture of direct quotes and reporting. The main task in this activity is to decide on some conventions for choosing between reporting or quoting in newspaper reports.

Before you begin the activity, write down some of your reasons for the choices writers make.

Bard 'is too tough for today's pupils' (Activity 2.10)
1) What pattern of reporting and quoting is established when each person is referred to for their opinions on the problem?
2) Why do you think the writer has selected the quotes reproduced in the text?

Fishermen survive six months adrift (Activity 2.13)
There is only one direct quote in this text. Suggest reasons for this.

Mike plunges in to save girl (Activity 2.31)
Most of this text is quoted from the rescuer. Why do you think that this is the case?

Woman sets up con at guest house (Activity 2.31)
Which people are quoted in this text? Why do you think the reporter has made this choice?

Further ideas

Quoting and reporting: the choice
Imagine you are a journalist. You interview a person about a particular incident which they witnessed. You tape record the interview and transcribe it. When preparing your report you take extracts from the interview and report them. Other extracts are taken directly from the transcript. Why do you choose to report some things and quote others?

1) *Directness*   If you quote directly, your report will appear more 'personal', more 'alive' and more direct, as if the reader is listening to the witness.
2) *Interpretation*   When we report, the choice of reporting verb and then how we choose to encode what a person has said allows

for interpretation by the reporter. Of course, it is easy to misquote or to infer too much from what a person has said.

3) *Image*   If you, the reporter, want to make the witness seem foolish, you might quote directly a *selection* from what they say. Alternatively you might want to imply that the witness is truthful. Select that which makes them appear honest, and quote it.

4) *'Sound bites'*   Many political speeches are written as a series of 'sound bites' – one or two sentences which can be quoted to sum up the message of the speech in question.

There may be other factors involved in making this choice. A conventional grammatical account of direct and indirect speech will not deal with these factors – like so much in language study, we end up relying on our own knowledge and intuition, or making our implicit understanding explicit. (But don't quote me on that!)

3

ENGLISH IN DISCOURSE

Introduction

In Chapter 2 the activities concentrated on the exploration of various aspects of English grammar, or the basic systems of the language. Knowledge of and sensitivity towards the way in which the systems operate and are employed in everyday use is central to an awareness of language.

Chapter 3 provides an opportunity to explore other aspects of English usage, with the primary aim of raising awareness about various aspects of English as a system for communicating social meaning and conceptual meaning. This exploration will involve some engagement with the lexicon of English, pragmatics (the study of language use in social context) and discourse analysis (the study of how language is used to create broad interpersonal meanings through conversation and written text).

Figure 3.1 – based on Halliday's (1973) 'macrofunctions' – details the relationships between the three macrofunctions (textual, ideational and interpersonal) and the areas to which Chapter 3 provides an introduction. This chapter also invites readers to collect their own samples of language use – written and spoken – in order to do their own analyses. It is important to note that, while there is not necessarily a simple solution or answer to any question on language and language use, the questions posed by an examination of language in use are even more open ended than those posed by an investigation of grammar. Because the listener's and the reader's interpretation is always the central focus of this work, it is important that readers become accustomed to making their own judgements about language in use, and to be aware of the basis of their own interpretations.

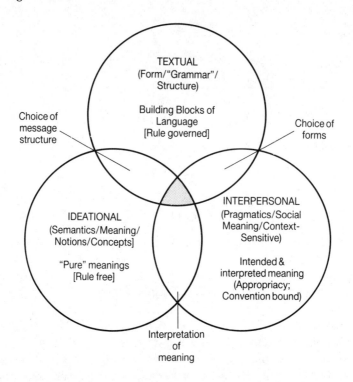

FIG. 3.1 Halliday's (1973) macrofunctions (acknowledgements to Chris Candlin, Lancaster, 1981)

Lexis: patterns

Aim   To examine the basic patterns of lexis and lexical use in texts.

ACTIVITY 3.1

Patterns in vocabulary

Examine the list of words which follows and arrange them according to the relationships in meaning that you see between them. What different sorts of meaning relationship can you find? Are there any odd ones out – items which seem to have no relationship with the others? Put these in a separate list and note any specific characteristics they possess.

massive	open	elephant	wearily
tiny	trudge	lorry	sleepily
happy	close	animal	rapidly
outrageous	run	van	sadly
astonishing	walk	car	silently
skinny	gallop	taxi	
smelly	climb	donkey	
awkward	creep	bicycle	
stubborn	rush	vehicle	
expensive	accelerate	horse	
intelligent	drive	tank	
silly	stop	llama	

Thinking questions
1) What patterns of lexis have you found in this exercise? Give examples.
2) Are there any ways in which lexical patterns overlap with grammatical patterns? Give examples from the word list.

ACTIVITY 3.2

Same word – different meaning?
How many meanings for the following items can you find?

leg	top	pick	nail	branch	arm

Can you add to the list other lexical items with the same sorts of variation in meaning? (maximum 5.)
   If you are a non-native speaker of English, or know another language well: are there similar variations in the L2 equivalents of these words in either your native language or the second language you know?

Thinking question
How are we able to understand the meaning carried by a word of the type above?

ACTIVITY 3.3

Collocations: words that go together
A)   Match the words in the two columns in as many ways as you can.

witty	joke
laughable	story
hilarious	anecdote
funny	one-liner
amusing	news
rib-tickling	argument
ridiculous	speech
bizarre	lecture
dirty	quip

B)   List as many possible combinations as you can with the verbs *do* and *pick*, to form expressions or idioms. For example, to *do* the cooking; to *pick* someone to pieces

Are there any other verbs in English, like *do* and *pick*, which form many expressions?
C)   It depends . . .

1)   Why do such expressions as 'He's complacent' 'She's naive' and 'He's dogmatic' imply criticism?
2)   Explain the differences between the use of the word *revolutionary* in the following sentences.

It's a *revolutionary* concept in motoring pleasure.
She's a real *revolutionary* – very dangerous, too.
The policy on environmental conservation is *revolutionary*.

Thinking questions
1)   What have you learned about the connection between lexis and meaning in English from doing these tasks?
2)   How do you think new expressions come into fashion and use? Can you say anything about the way these expressions seem to develop using insights from any of these activities?

ACTIVITY 3.4

Who's speaking, where and to whom?
Explain the circumstances under which the following exchanges could be interpreted as misunderstandings or breakdowns in communication.

1) A: Charming little brats, aren't they?
   B: How dare you!
2) A: He had an appendectomy yesterday, didn't you know?
   B: I didn't notice anything personally.
3) A: Is there a rest-room around here?
   B: There's a waiting-room just over there.
4) A: Nice bird you've got there, Luigi.
   B: No, this is my girlfriend.
5) A: (Male teacher, entering class): Good morning everyone.
   B: (Students): Hi, mate.
6) A: There isn't sufficient milk for breakfast.
   B: Then you'd better go and purchase some, hadn't you?

Thinking questions
Has communication broken down in the extracts above? What influence has the use of individual words on any breakdowns or misunderstandings. Do any breakdowns have a deeper meaning?

ACTIVITY 3.5

Idioms
Which of these idioms do you think are easiest to understand? Why?

tip of my tongue
raining cats and dogs
on a sticky wicket
sleep like a log
get the sack
kick someone up in the air
out of the blue
get the ball rolling
pull someone's leg

Thinking questions
What do you notice about the construction of these idioms? What do you notice about the use of lexis in these idioms?

Further ideas

Lexis: patterns of form

All lexical items have formal elements. These include prefixes and suffixes, as well as the 'root' of a word. Prefixes provide important elements of meaning (negative, repetition, etc.). Suffixes provide information about the grammatical class of a word in many cases. The suffix '–er', however, can cause problems. In *sniper* it converts *snipe* to a noun, but it is not a suffix in *winter*. Although knowledge of the system of prefixes and suffixes is helpful in understanding meaning, we should be on our guard for exceptions to any generalizations we might make. Look back over the word list in Activity 3.1 for examples of interesting formal patterns in the words, as in *sniper* and *winter*.

Lexis consists of more than words, however. In complex idioms and expressions, a complete phrase is often used – the lexical item must, therefore, be the whole phrase. The meaning is derived from the combination of the items. The same applies to so-called 'phrasal verbs' (see p. 89).

Knowing how English words are 'built' may also enable us to say something about their origin. Latinate roots, for example, are very common in English words – with a knowledge of Latin, or a Latin-based language like French or Italian, a student can unpick the meanings of many words.

Compounding has also become common in English. This is where a complex noun phrase (in a large number of instances) becomes a single item. For example, 'table lamp' or 'washing machine' are lexical items in their own right, although a dictionary will not have entries for these except as combinations of headwords (see p. 68 and p. 97).

TASKS

1)   Scan through a copy of a magazine or newspaper and note unusual words or lexical items. Are the items connected with particular activities such as sport? Note the use of words which are not English – are there specific conventions for their use, for example, use of parentheses or italic?

2)   Think of some famous twentieth-century figures – in the fields of science, politics, the arts. Make a list. How many of their names have been used to create new lexical items? Check your ideas against an up-to-date dictionary (for example, with the suffix '-ism' or '-ite').

Vocabulary choices in written texts

Aim   To investigate the various ways in which lexis is used to create meanings in texts, and how different contexts contribute to different meanings.

ACTIVITY 3.6

Read the text which follows. As you do so, underline all the lexical items which have a connection with the word *asleep* (line 1). Indicate whether the connection of the lexical item with *asleep* is direct or indirect, and how much your own personal interpretation of the connection is involved. Then write the items out on a separate piece of paper as a chain of words. What do you notice about the chain? Now arrange the items in a different way, for example, a web, with *asleep* at the centre. What decisions have you made about the juxtaposition of the items? Finally, try to write your own text without reference to the original, based either on your chain or your other arrangement of the items.

> Why we spend a third of our lives *asleep*, no one really knows. We sleep for almost twenty years in a lifetime – a considerable period to lie almost immobile, remote from the waking world, rising and falling in waves of emotional experience that are mostly forgotten. It is astonishing that we can succumb to sleep with so little curiosity. We submit to hours of stillness, passively allowing the motive forces of our personalities and the regenerative cycles of our bodies to prepare us for daily birth, to fertilise our waking minds and memories with haunting shadows of the people we really are. All of humankind participates in this mysterious rhythm. The daily recurrence of sleep, like the tides of the seas, suggests that it has rhythmic importance to us, but someone is always hoping to find that sleep is expendable. Every year newspapers report that some ancient man or woman, usually in a remote corner of Spain or Japan, has never slept. When sleep scientists have investigated they have never found the person who never sleeps. It is easier to forgo food for several weeks than sleep. After only forty-eight hours without sleep most people experience an inability to sustain attention or to remember what they have just heard, and fragments of dreams or reverie begin to intrude on their waking activity (Luce, 1973: 67–68).

Thinking question
How far do you think our understanding of a written text is related to our ability to 'follow' chains of lexis in a text?

ACTIVITY 3.7

Note   Cover set text on p. 146 before carrying out the next activity.

1) What do you think will be the subject of a text with the following items in it?

children   parental discipline   chopsticks   clumsy Westerners
training to think   balancing   improvement   traditionalists

Write down what you think will be the subject of the text.

2) Read the text which follows and identify the items you predicted before you were given the text. Does the text conform to the predictions you made? In what ways does it confound your predictions?

Doom seen in crumbling of chopstick culture

Kevin Rafferty in Tokyo

Japanese children are becoming so *undisciplined* and used to sloppy Western ways of eating that barely 10 per cent of primary school pupils up to the
5 age of 10 know how to use chopsticks properly.

A new survey has *alarmed* traditionalists. The inability to use chopsticks, they say, not only shows poor *manners*
10 but demonstrates declining parental discipline and *bodes ill* for Japan's economic future.

Akira Murakoshi, chief secretary of the Children's Life Science Research
15 Group, quotes a Japanese *saying*: 'Takaga hashi, saredo hashi – It's not just a chopstick, it's important to life.'

The survey showed that among children to the age of 10, a mere 10.6 per
20 cent could use chopsticks in the approved *manner*. Among older children there was some *improvement*, but not much. By contrast, a 1936 study found some 75 per cent of infants
25 aged 3½ could use chopsticks; today the figure is less than 1 per cent.

To use chopsticks correctly, the thumb, *index* and third fingers are employed, with the fourth finger for
30 balancing. The controlling finger is the third, not the index finger, which many *clumsy* Westerners try to use.

This ability to use tools sets man apart from monkeys, says Kisou
35 Kubota, of Kyoto University. 'To make the chopsticks *function*, you must think. And that becomes training to think, seek solutions and move forward' (*Guardian*, 16 June 1992).

3)   Create synonyms for the words *italicized* in the text. Would substituting them for the words in the text at the appropriate point change the meaning of the text in any ways?

4)   Now analyse the text according to 'sets' of lexical items which seem to have common themes or ideas connecting them. Can you find 'chains' of lexical items in the text? Does the text seem to develop according to the nature of the lexical chains?

5)   Try to identify a 'pivot' item in the text from which all other items seem to radiate. Try drawing a conceptual map of how the text is structured from the pivot item. What do you learn about text structure from this exercise?

Thinking questions
How far do you agree with the notion that the meaning of lexical items extends far beyond the boundaries of words when they are used in texts? What evidence do you have? Refer to the texts in Activities 3.6 and 3.7.

ACTIVITY 3.8

Identify the ways in which the use of lexical items creates links in meaning between different parts of the texts which follow. Circle the lexical items which are linked and think about the nature of the links.

1) Mistake revealed in secret evidence
Sir Robert Armstrong, the Cabinet Secretary, yesterday admitted giving wrong and misleading evidence on what has been one of the key issues in the MI5 secrets case.

2) An epidemic of influenza is sweeping the European areas of the Soviet Union, despite a mass vaccination programme carried out last September.
   Up to a third of the staff of Moscow Radio were off work this week with flu, Western correspondents in Moscow have been told.

3) The French Prime Minister, M. Jacques Chirac, shaken by mass student demonstrations, decided yesterday to withdraw a controversial government bill introducing selection to universities, in a surprise climbdown.
   The retreat was disclosed soon after the Universities Minister, M. Alain Devaquet, had defended his reforms in parliament...

4) After eight years under construction the new Paris Orsay Museum, dedicated to the nineteenth century, received its first visitors yesterday in what used to be a mainline railway station.
   The 700-ft long building on the Seine's Left Bank was in service until 1939...

5) A.   Our next-door neighbour is very brusque; I can't stand the man.
   B.   The lions and leopards were short of food, a fate which can befall any animal.
   C.   This knife's blunt. What can we do about the thing?
   D.   Mud was everywhere – the stuff was on your feet, your clothes, even in your hair.
   E.   There seems no end to the Iran arms deal affair.
   F.   They all bought shares. It seemed a good move at the time.
   G.   Have you any ideas about what to do in Paris? I've never been to the place.
   H.   Bill seems to be certain that he can make money selling crockery. I don't know where he got the idea from.

6) There's a man running over there . . .
   A.   The man's going to fall over if he isn't careful.
   B.   Those men are always out jogging.
   C.   And there's another running on the other side of the road.
   D.   More men should take exercise.

Thinking questions

How do the types of links between lexical items which you have found above enable you to understand the meaning of the texts? Would there be a change in meaning if the links were different, or if there were different lexical items used?

ACTIVITY 3.9

Refer to the texts noted below.

Woman sets up con at guest house (Activity 2.31)
1) List all the words in the text which refer to *crime*, the *law* and its *procedures*, and *personal problems*. Do you see any overlap between the items in each list? What does this tell you about (a) lexis as it is used in texts and (b) relationships between various lexical items?
2) Lines 9–10 – 'won the sympathy of'; line 15 – 'stalled their payments'; line 34 – 'fed with bulletins': Comment on these expressions in terms of their meaning as 'chunks' of meaning, and the components of each one.
3) What do you think would be the effect if the reporter had decided to report the parts which are quoted? Would the reporter have used a different lexical set?

Naipaul (Activity 2.43)
1) List all items in the text with a *political* connection, all items which relate to *work* and *employment* and all items which refer to *social* life. Are any items

shared between the lists? How do these items contribute to the meaning and the message of the text?

2) 'If you understand the vocabulary, you understand the message of a text.' Discuss this claim with reference to the text.

3) Find compound words in the text. What do you notice about the way they are formed?

4) List all the descriptive words the author uses. How do these contribute to the message of the text? What is the effect of (a) removing them from the text and (b) replacing them with synonyms?

Further ideas

Lexis – patterns of meaning and use

We are all quite familiar with the idea that lexical items have synonyms (items with similar meanings) and antonyms (items with an opposite meaning). Words also form hyponomous sets – a hyponym like *vegetable* has many items under its general meaning, such as *carrot, cabbage, potato*, etc. Ultimately, words congregate in semantic fields: broad areas of meaning which share common characteristics. Theories of cognition (e.g., Neisser, 1976) emphasize the importance of *schemata* – which are both means of storing concepts in the brain and also means of actively interpreting the world. Schemata are very important for storing lexical items, and processing language data.

Patterns of meaning in a text are more complex, however. The *use* of lexis depends on a wide range of variables, drawing on patterns of form and meaning. But the author would then think about an audience for any piece of text, spoken or written, the setting in which the text will be created, and so on. In use, we draw on our knowledge of such features as collocation, but are much more sensitive to the connotations of lexical items, and the potential *effect* of words on listeners and speakers. We can elect to be formal or informal with our selection of words; we can choose to be rude or polite and so on. *Choice* is the essential feature of lexical use. Texts are the results of choices at many levels – lexical choice is a central choice.

TASKS

1) When an author's language is described as 'rich' it is usually the choice of lexical items that is at issue. Choose one or two authors of fiction and study their use of lexis. Make judgements about the 'richness' of the prose on the basis of their use of lexis.

2) Find the same news story in two or three different newspapers. Compare the use of lexis in the three accounts, by using the 'semantic field' technique you practised in Activity 3.9. Choose three or four headings and put the lexical

items from the texts under each heading. Compare the texts in this way and look for overlaps between the messages of the texts and the sets of lexical items.

Investigating texts

Aim   To investigate various aspects of written texts.

ACTIVITY 3.10

Organizing texts

1)   Read and compare the two versions of the same story which follow. In what ways do they differ? Which version is the 'easier' to comprehend? Which do you prefer, and why? What specific features of written language are exemplified in the different texts? (e.g., ordering of events, sentence structures).

A.   A driver who raced along a West German motorway had a lucky escape when his sports car hit a crash barrier and took off over the tree-tops, police in Bonn said yesterday. The Greek driver clambered from the wreckage when his car crash-landed in a wood.

B.   The police in Bonn said that on a German motorway a Greek driver crashed in his sports car. He was racing along a motorway and took off over the tree-tops. He hit a crash barrier and crash-landed in a wood. He clambered from the wreckage and had a lucky escape.

Thinking question

What does the organization of a text contribute to its meaning? Refer to the texts above.

2)   Study the following text and comment on the way in which it is organized. If you think it can be improved, try to rewrite it.

For life in the sand, the Sand Boa is well fitted. For pushing down below the surface, its head is wedge-shaped; from the head to the very short tail, which ends in a blunt point and is therefore much feared by the local people, the body is more or less the same thickness. With irregular brownish patches of varying size, the colour is a pale yellow or orange. Being in about 40 rows around the middle of the body, the scales are small and numerous; they are also quite smooth, and this character, with the small head, which is not at all distinct from the body, makes the Sand Boa easily distinguishable from the very venomous sand-living vipers. Though Mueller's Sand Boa, the one most likely to be met, reaches only 20 in., some reach a length of up to 30 in. (adapted from Cansdale, 1961: 22–3).

Thinking question
What aspects of the text have you altered? Why? What is the effect of the changes?

ACTIVITY 3.11

Links in texts
Read through the pairs of sentences and comment on the connections between them. What features of each of the sentences enable you to draw these conclusions? Is there anything else which might help you draw conclusions from the pairs of sentences? What helps you to interpret them?

1) The Prime Minister took the platform. Her speech was hard-hitting.
2) Rosie went to get the kids' toys from the car. The boot was locked.
3) Peter's going to Paris next week. I hope the rail strike is over by then.
4) I found the old watch. The strap had rotted.
5) He bought a ten-speed racer. He really likes cycling.
6) The cat scratched the little girl. My mother caught the cat and held it until the vet arrived.
7) He got hold of a really good book on Saturday. It was only £2.99 in the sale.
8) That's a brilliant new record. It confirms his position as No. 1 in Britain at the moment.

Thinking question
There is an argument which states that it is a reader's interpretation of a text, while reading, that is the key factor in creating the meaning of the text – in other words, meaning is mainly created by the reader.

Do you think that writers actually lay down clues to potential meaning in the way they structure texts? Look at Activities 3.10 and 3.11 in order to help you think about the question.

ACTIVITY 3.12

Choose one of the groups of titles and paragraph headings, either A, B, C or D. Then read the accompanying text with these in mind. What features of the text support the title and headings you are working with?

Then choose one of the other sets and read the text again. How far is your second reading influenced by the headings and how far by a reinterpretation of the text based on the new headings?

Now choose the set of headings you prefer and note your reasons for your choice.

A)   THE GEOGRAPHY OF BRITISH GUIANA
1)   From Trinidad to South America
2)   The Coastal Area of British Guiana
3)   The Interior of British Guiana
B)   A MISERABLE COUNTRY
1)   From the Beauty of Trinidad to the Ugliness of South America
2)   The Overcrowded Coastal Strip
3)   The Unending Boredom of the Interior
C)   A COLONIAL MISTAKE
1)   Gentle Trinidad/Remote South America
2)   The Organized and Developed Coastal Strip
3)   The Untouched Interior
D)   A FAILURE
1)   Freshness and Decay
2)   The Seeds of Unrest
3)   A Wasted Land

1.   From the air Trinidad's Atlantic coast was outlined as on the map, the waves steadily rolling lace-patterned foam towards the shore, green edged with yellow. The waves began far out and rolled in evenly. On the bright blue water cloud shadows were like submerged rocks or like dissolving drops of ink. Soon blue water turned to brown, its progressively darker shades neatly contoured and sometimes marked off in white. Then the South American continent: a grey-green tufted carpet, worn brown in patches, with rivers like cracks in drying mud. For minute after minute we moved rapidly over the unchanging, unwelcoming land, a small corner of a vast continent, where trees grew and collapsed on muddy shores.

2.   One can learn much about British Guiana from the air: its size, its emptiness, the isolation of its communities. Six hundred thousand people live in a country the size of Britain, and when you fly over the populated eastern coastal strip you see why there is so much unrest in a country, which from its bigness, should be a country of opportunity. The land here is fertile. The sugarcane fields, intersected by ruler-straight ditches, are like machine-made carpets. They go on and on, until the pattern is broken by a huddle of white-and-rust wooden houses, laid out as precisely as the fields: workers' houses: sugarcane land, you feel, going to waste, and the site arbitrarily chosen, for the settlement could have been put down anywhere else in that clear green expanse. 'To force the Negroes of the Virgin Islands to work,' Michael Swan writes in *The Marches of El Dorado*, the Danes cut down their soursop trees, and today in British

Guiana sugar must use a hundred subtle methods to maintain a sufficient labour force – tropical people prefer a subsistence and little work to hard work and a higher standard of living.'

3.   And emptiness. Fly to the interior. First you go over the sugarcane fields beside the brown Demerara River. Abruptly the fields stop and bush begins; and in the bush there are little irregular areas of timorous destruction – indicating attitudes you will learn to associate with British Guiana – where forest has turned to marshland, for the soil here is poor and hardwood trees cannot easily be made to grow again. Within minutes towns, fields and clearings are passed, and you are over the forest, thick and choked and even, occasionally flawed by a river that is black or, when caught by the sun, glinting, a vein of gold or red through the dead green. And the forest continues. You cease to look, until, thirty or forty minutes later, the land breaks up into hills and valleys, beyond which lie the savannah lands, in the dry season marbled in green and brown and ochre, scratched with white trails, the beds of diminished streams lined with rich, succulent-looking palm trees. Brazil is not far away, equally empty, a vastness not to be comprehended (Naipaul, 1963: 92–93).

Thinking questions
What have you discovered in this activity about

1) the structure of texts and the themes and subject matter of texts;
2) the contribution of the author's lexical and grammatical choices to the development of themes in texts; and
3) the contribution of a reader's ideas and knowledge to the development and interpretation of a text?

Further ideas

Readers create meanings from texts. What an author intends is not necessarily the same as what the reader interprets. So how does an author attempt to give the reader a lead in coming to appreciate the author's intended meaning? An author can do this in several ways:

1) Repetition of lexical items or sentence patterns to emphasize a point or argument.
2) 'Loading' sentences in specific ways – front loading with adverbials tends to weaken statements, whereas end loading tends to emphasize the importance of the fronted element of a sentence. Subsequent parts of a sentence have the effect of afterthoughts regardless of whether or not they are the main clause.
3) The ordering of the events or ideas in a text, and their juxtaposition, can give important, if oblique, messages to a reader. Beginning a text with 'The police said', rather than 'Yesterday there was an accident' is likely

to set up different expectations in readers about the content and attitude of the text. (Fairclough, 1989, has interesting and relevant ideas on this point.) Part of the author/speaker's problem is always either to confirm or disconfirm the initial expectations set up in the listener or reader's mind at the beginning of a piece of discourse.

Discourse is a subtle process of negotiating between specifying a point of view and allowing the reader or listener to catch what they can from the text and develop their own interpretation. Structuring and organizational conventions are the basic tools at a speaker or writer's disposal when they create a text. Discourse analysis in part tries to identify and understand these conventions.

Spoken and written

Aim　To investigate the differences between spoken and written text.

ACTIVITY 3.13

1)　List what you think are the main differences between spoken and written language.

2)　Read the two texts which follow. They both refer to the same topic; the first is the transcript of a spontaneous spoken report, and the second is a written report of the same incident.

What major differences do you find between the two texts? Refer to your categories established in 1) above and add any new ones that either of the two texts exhibits.

A. walked down there about an hour ago to have a look/and/it is/it looks as if a bomb's hit it/there are caravans upside down/erhm/some on their sides/some of them have been completely ripped away from the/area anyway/er/and I understand from the people that erm/that the actual people that live in them/is that the/er/chassis/ /which are actually chained down to concrete/er/the top part of the caravan has been ripped away from the chassis in a lot of instances/and it's just bowled over and over across the field.

B. I walked down there about an hour ago to have a look, and it looks as if a bomb's hit it. There are caravans upside down and on their sides. I understand from the people who live in them that the top part of the caravan has, in a lot of instances, been ripped away from the chassis, which is actually chained down to the concrete, and been bowled over and over across the field.

Note   / signifies a pause in the transcript of the spoken text. (Activity inspired by Brown and Yule, 1983.)

Thinking questions
1) What are the implications for making judgements about people's spoken language on the basis of this activity? (What sorts of judgement do we tend to make?)
2) Is it true to say that the spoken form of the language is a more 'basic' form than the written form? Is written language 'grammaticized speech'?

ACTIVITY 3.14

Organize the eight sentences which follow in an order which creates a paragraph that 'reads smoothly' and 'makes sense'.

As you create the paragraph, note down the clues and strategies which enabled you to arrange the sentences successfully and also any problems you encountered.

1) The pattern is changing: the power of the chiefs and the emirs is being eroded by the politicians, while the business tycoons are emerging as a new aristocracy.
2) There, the French, with their zeal for exporting French civilisation, left an isolated elite, which was more French than African, and largely divorced from the populace.
3) Literature, both in English and the Nigerian languages, has flourished here as in no other African country; so have drama, music and sculpture.
4) Nigeria is more confidently African than its ex-French neighbours, like the Ivory Coast or Benin.
5) But, even in change, it remains completely Nigerian.
6) In those countries, much of the administration and most of the big business are still in French hands; hotels, small butchers' shops and even cafes are owned and run by French people.
7) Government at the local level, which is the level that matters to people, is shaped by traditional institutions.
8) Nigerian life, on the other hand, is African in all departments and at all levels.

(Parry 1979: 5)

Thinking questions
Has the experience of doing this activity added to or modified any of your knowledge about textual organization? If so, in what ways?

ACTIVITY 3.15

A)   Link the sentences which follow into a paragraph of text. Before you do so, it might help to imagine a potential reader of your text. The reader may be native speaker, non-native speaker, old, young, etc.

1)   *Tyrannosaurus rex* was a very fierce creature.
2)   No other creature was as fierce as *Tyrannosaurus rex*.
3)   It stood nearly 8 metres high.
4)   It weighed about 5 tonnes.
5)   It was a meat-eater.
6)   It hunted smaller reptiles.
7)   It lived on the grasslands.
8)   *Tyrannosaurus rex* was the king of the dinosaurs.
9)   It stood on its hind legs.
10) Its teeth were over 10 centimetres long.
11) Its teeth were ideal for cutting meat.

Thinking questions
Have you had to change the order of the sentences? What devices have you used to link the sentences? Whom do you think your text might be read by? How far has your perception of a particular reader influenced the way in which you have organized your text?

B)   Look at the text which follows. Do you think it is an 'authentic' text? Would you want to change it in any way? If so, what are your reasons for wanting to change it? Who do you think wrote it – what are your reasons for your conclusions?

> I am a wild lion and I live in the mountains. I hunt for antelopes and buffaloes and other small animals. And there are other big animals in the jungles in the mountains and I live in East Africa. And I live in a cave in East Africa. I live all alone in the mountains. Cheetahs, leopards and rhino and giraffes live near me. I am yellow and I have a brown mane.

C)   What changes (if any) would you want to make to the following text in order to make it suitable for a group of young learners (either native or non-native speakers)? Would you provide any other assistance to the learner? (Exercise inspired by Hawkins, 1987.)

> **Carnivora** (*Zool.*) An order of primarily carnivorous Mammals, terrestrial or aquatic; usually with three pairs of incisors in each jaw and large prominent canines; the last upper premolar and the first lower molar frequently modified as carnassial teeth; collar bone reduced or absent; four or five unguiculate

digits on each limb. Cats, Lions, Tigers, Panthers, Dogs, Wolves, Jackals, Bears, Raccoons, Skunks, Seals, Sea-Lions and Walruses (*Chambers Science and Technology Dictionary*, 1991: 187).

Thinking questions

Summarize what you have discovered about the organization and structure of written and spoken discourse from this set of activities.

What are the implications of your discoveries for (1) teaching English, (2) writing and (3) reading newspapers? Do you think you will be more critically alert when you read or listen having done these activities? If so, in which ways?

Further ideas

Written text is more 'rigid' than spoken text. Speakers have the opportunity of correcting themselves, of back-tracking, of repeating themselves in the presence of the listener, and in response to the listener's feedback. Writers do not have the advantage of self-correction, although they can back-track or repeat themselves. Their text stands or falls without their being present when the reader reads. There is potential for misinterpretation, misunderstanding and so on. In anticipation of this, written text is generally more tightly organized than spoken text.

It is interesting to observe the tendency of newspapers to adopt a more 'spoken' mode of presentation these days. The language is more 'informal'; there is more quoting and less reporting. The 'soundbite' (the extract from a political speech which is considered instantly memorable, common in political discourse in Britain and particularly the USA) and the apparent need to produce chunks of easily digestible text for listeners and readers is partly responsible. Additionally, a 'spoken' format is more likely to appeal directly to a reader. Gossip is a basic social need of human groups – it is 'loosely organized', open-ended, subject to inconclusiveness. Thus, important news is given by 'sound bite' and other news is gossip-like.

TASKS

1) Study different newspapers in order to verify or disprove the assertions made above. Do the same with the television and radio news.

2) Collect tape-recordings of people speaking as naturally as possible about various topics. Transcribe some and see if you can add to your list of features of spoken language.

Language use in social contexts

Aim   To investigate how language is used in specific social contexts and to discover some of the conventions that underlie language use.

ACTIVITY 3.16

A teacher friend of mine recently received an invitation to go to a party held by a group of his students. Unfortunately, the party was at a time at which it was impossible for my friend to attend. So he decided to write and turn down the invitation. It was not as easy as he had thought it would be! He realized he was not at all sure how to respond: he had a pressing family commitment but did not want to offend the students in any way. Here are some of the thoughts that came to him while writing. He began his reply like this: 'Thanks ever so much for inviting me to your party next week.' But how to decline the invitation?

Here are some of the alternatives he considered in order to continue the letter. Which one do you think he eventually chose? And why? Would you choose a different way of declining? If so, how would you do it? Why reject some of the alternatives below?

1)   Unfortunately, I can't come because of family commitments.
2)   I can't make it, I'm afraid.
3)   I'm doing something else on that particular evening, I'm afraid.
4)   Unfortunately, I can't come because my daughter is in a school play on that evening, and I've promised her I'll attend.
5)   Regrettably, I cannot attend.
6)   I must inform you that I am unable to attend due to unforeseen circumstances.
7)   What a pity that I won't be able to come.
8)   I'm very honoured. But unfortunately I have a prior engagement.
9)   Sorry, but I can't come on that particular evening.
10)   I wish I could come, but I'm already busy on that evening.

Thinking questions   List the factors which have influenced your choice of response. What does your choice tell you about your attitudes to language use? How far do you think that these factors apply to all instances of communication? Would, for instance, your friends and colleagues do the same?

ACTIVITY 3.17

A)   Divide the following sentences into two groups, according to the meaning of the main verb, giving reasons for your decisions:

I agree with you.
I feed the cat every morning.
I play hockey.
I conclude that you're wrong.
I reject your idea.
I cycle to work.
I protest.
I maintain that she's right.
I question her motives.

B)   Explain the difference between 'I do' in the following:

1)   X: Who likes Whitney Houston?
      Y: I do.
2)   X: Do you take this man to be your lawfully wedded husband?
      Y: I do.
3)   X: You don't like her. I can see that.
      Y: I do.

C)   When a witness says 'I do' while being sworn in during a court sequence, what conditions must prevail in order for it to fulfil its function?
      Consider the following:

what has already been said
how it was said
who is present
who says what to whom
when it can be uttered

Does the utterance 'Objection' in a courtroom require the same type of conditions in order to fulfil its intended function?

Thinking question
Do you know any other expressions like 'I do' which seem to perform a number of different functions?

D)   Distinguish between the following utterances by trying to insert 'hereby' before the main verb in each one. Which ones allow 'hereby' to be inserted?

1)   I apologize to you.
2)   I know you.
3)   I testify that I saw the accident.
4)   I suspect that she saw the accident.
5)   I bid you welcome.

6) I resign.
7) I repeat.
8) I beg you to help.

Now try putting 'am willing to' before the main verb in each utterance. Is there any change in meaning? What is the effect?

Thinking questions
1) What particular social contexts or activities are characterized by the language use you have been investigating in this sequence of activities: How would you describe this use of language?
2) 'Everything a person says is underpinned by a speech act.' Thus 'You're great' contains the speech act 'I state . . .', 'I believe . . .', or 'I state that you're great.' How far do the examples in this series of exercises bear this proposition out?

Further ideas

Matching language choices to contexts
Social embarrassment can occur when we fail to match our language choice to the social situation. We may misread the status relationships between participants and ourselves – we may behave too closely or too distantly, for example. The situation might be fairly informal, but we read it as formal: we come across as being 'stiff' or unfriendly. We might also be ignorant of the conventions for addressing someone older than ourselves, and fail to accord them sufficient respect. These are common enough occurrences, but important enough to dwell upon, none the less.

Social awareness and language use are very intimately related. However, because none of us can know the conventions of every social setting, we are likely to make mistakes, linguistically and in our associated behaviour. Thus crosscultural encounters, encounters between different age groups, social groups, or even occupational groups are often fraught with potential for the *faux pas* or 'social mistake'. Knowing the conventions is a mark of group membership and therefore social identity. Every language user has a knowledge of these conventions for his or her own social circles. Success in encounters outside these circles depends on being able to interact and, at the same time, observe, listen and ask insiders. It is a set of conventions to which we never stop adding during our lives. Many great jokes are derived from turning the conventions upside down. Oscar Wilde made a successful career as a playwright partly by satirizing people's sensibilities to 'manners'.

A central aspect of understanding language use is, therefore, understanding the multitude of factors that influence its use in various social situations.

ACTIVITY 3.18

Look at the A/B exchanges which follow and try to work out what B thinks A means on the basis of what B's reply is in each case. Do any of B's responses seem strange in any way? Note the ways in which they seem to be unusual or unexpected.

What do you think A might say (or do) as a result of what B says? (In other words, what do you think A might infer from B's utterance in each case?)

1) A: I see Bill's got a new job.
   B: The unemployment situation is getting worse.
2) A: We'll really miss them.
   B: Well, I'll miss Paul.
3) A: Mrs Biggs is a right old cow.
   B: I hear that the Stock Exchange has crashed.
4) A: Is 'B' the right answer?
   B: You're getting warmer.
5) A: Has anybody seen Roger around?
   B: There's a red car by the library.
6) A: She picked up Spanish ever so quickly.
   B: Her French is good, isn't it?
7) A: You ought to be more careful in future.
   B: I'm trying my best.
8) A: Do you have cooking oil?
   B: Large or small?

Thinking questions
Do you think that these exchanges obey or disobey certain social or cultural rules? Can you state any of these rules? Would these rules prove a barrier to a non-native speaker's learning English?

ACTIVITY 3.19

A)   Write down five possible replies to the following question, noting the sorts of contextual information you are assuming. Try to include both direct and indirect responses as well as polite and impolite responses. Is there a correspondence between polite and the indirect responses?

Can I borrow your Walkman?

Your replies
1)

2)

3)

4)

5)

B)   In the following exchanges, decide whether A or B is being impolite. If so, in which ways are A and/or B being impolite? What contextual knowledge are you assuming?

1) A: That was a really interesting talk you gave there.
   B: Yes. It really got them thinking.
2) A: You will help me with my assignment, won't you?
   B: You haven't started it yet I suppose.
3) A: You ought to hear my new record. It's great.
   B: Well . . . jazz doesn't really turn me on that much.
4) A: Do you know anything more about the arrangements for this summer?
   B: There's a meeting next week.
5) A: What a lovely job you've made of the decorations.
   B: There's still a lot to do and some of it . . . shall we say could be better.
   A: But it's much better than I could do.
6) A: Can you tell me the way to High Street?
   B: You're in it.

What conversational principles (or maxims) might have been flouted in these examples in order to be polite or rude (or otherwise)? Which force do you think is stronger in conversation, the desire to state one's intentions or needs, or the desire to be polite? What 'rules' underlie your ideas?

C)   In order to test your ideas about directness and indirectness in speech, examine the six utterances which follow, and try to grade them from most to least direct in terms of their being *requests*. (You may need to provide a context to assist you.)

1) It's pretty wintery today.
2) It's a bit drafty in here, isn't it?
3) I like fresh air, but this is ridiculous.
4) Were you born in a field?

5) Put the wood in the hole.
6) The door's feeling insecure.

Thinking question
Do you think that there is a relationship between politeness and indirectness in speech?

Further ideas

According to Leech (1983), the choice to be polite or impolite, and the use of tact, irony and banter, are all subject to a cost/benefit calculation on the part of the speaker. This calculation is rarely made as overtly or crudely as a literal interpretation of Leech's ideas might lead us to believe. Because these choices are made in a matter of split seconds, one must assume remarkably complex cognitive operations proceeding in parallel – computation of the various parameters of the social context, decisions as to the *force* of the utterance (direct or indirect, persuading or ordering, for example), choice of the appropriate formal vehicle for the message, choice of lexical items. It is no wonder that 'communication is a risky business'! It is more surprising that we manage to communicate successfully even half the time. And this analysis does not include an affective or emotional element, which is difficult to analyse in cost/benefit terms. Yet we are all aware of the importance of 'good communication skills' in many occupations and in personal relationships. 'Good communicators' listen well – they are good judges of a conversation: they only interrupt when the speaker indicates that an intervention is appropriate for that stage in the conversation, for example.

All communication involves calculation on the part of speakers and listeners. But the calculations are 'natural' and usually spontaneous. How do we recognize lack of spontaneity? Or insincerity? There is more to communication than pragmatics has revealed so far. The implications for the ways in which we manage our organizations, teach and learn in classrooms, train people and run the affairs of state are manifold – the next stage of the development of linguistics could be to explore these dimensions.

ACTIVITY 3.20

Questions
A) Write down as many different *types* of question as you can. Give examples. Do they fall into categories? Does the type of question seem to depend on the purpose or goal of the question?
B) Examine the questions provided and try to decide on their type, according to your categories from A) above.

1) Isn't it funny the way they talk about you?
2) The place where they love you really is New York, isn't it?
3) Do you have superstitions?
4) Would you let your children play?
5) You're a rotten loser, aren't you?
6) Would you encourage anybody to be a professional tennis player . . . is it a good life?

C)   Study the short extracts from the transcript of a 'chat show' interview on television. Note how the speakers use conversational conventions. Are there any examples of impoliteness, or other 'flouts' of the conventions? Underline the questions A asks, as a way of addressing these issues.

(A is the interviewer or 'host'; B is the interviewee or 'guest'. What is A doing?)

A: Now, erm, it's great to see an old chap like yourself . . . still able to walk on . . . slowly but yeh.
B: I'm still making it casually though.
A: Isn't it funny the way they they talk about you . . . you're only 37 excuse me I'm a much older person but you're only 37 . . . for goodness sake and they talk about you as if you're about to die they say he should be giving up now he'll retire any moment and that was five years ago.

(How is B coping with A's questions?)

A: Do you hate those young players . . . yeh you do.
B: Well not if I was their age I wouldn't.
A: But you hate them I'd hate them . . . fellow like Agassi all that hair and funny shorts.
B: You're gonna get me into trouble here I can see that.
   . . .
A: Some of them are a bit brash though aren't they?

(Is B's response relevant?)

A: Have you any idea why we can't compete . . . is it something wrong with our attitude?
B: Well there's for sure nothing wrong with your talent.

Thinking question
What are the ways in which the speakers in the extracts above are both direct and indirect in the way they use language? Give examples.

Further ideas

Implications

When we read something or hear someone speak, we take decisions on the basis of what went before (if anything), what we think is coming, the content and form of what was said, and our understanding of the meaning of the utterance. We also work out the implications of what was said. While not everybody believes in conspiracy theory, speakers may not always mean precisely what they say. They may, like politicians trying not to offend supporters with an unpopular but necessary measure, 'speak in code'. Only the informed will be able to understand what exactly is meant. Adversaries usually understand each other better than they think because they second guess so much of what is to be said. The skill of political survival in a democracy may be partly due to being able to create messages from which people can draw their own meanings.

We are able as speakers and listeners to grasp subtle meanings of what people say because we have internalized the system for interpretation when people may be telling half-truths, or exaggerating, or being rude or coy. Without a knowledge of the conventions of communication, we would not be able to take part in social life beyond the strictly literal statement.

ACTIVITY 3.21

With reference to the transcripts provided, comment on the following:

1) How the participants appear to convey and interpret meanings in context.
2) How the participants appear to operate the conventions of conversation. (You might wish to state what these are before you begin.)
3) How the participants 'manage' the interactions using the turn-taking mechanism and other strategic devices.

You may wish to refine each of these categories in more detail before you start your work. For example, what sorts of features would you look for when thinking about how the speakers convey meaning? What conversational conventions are you examining? What 'management' mechanisms and devices are you examining?

Draw up a checklist of features to study. Go through the data systematically, following your checklist if necessary.

Extract 1 (Phone-in programme: Invicta Radio, Canterbury, Kent; A: Deejay; B: Caller.)

A: So who's your dedication for?
B: It's for Jan in Folkestone.

A: For who?

B: Jan.

A: Jan in Folkestone.

B: Yeah . . . I heard she wasn't very well . . . so I'm on me way.

A: OK, fine.

B: And can I, can I just say something about neigh . . . is that love call or is it Jim . . . wasn't he—

A: —yeah you could say that.

B: Love him, ha ha—

A: —he he.

B: Oh no hang on . . . he he . . . no about neighbours . . . people moan about foreigners moving in as neighbours.

A: Oh yeah—

B: —recently I've been doing some [*inaudible*]. I've just had an Eskimo move in next door to me.

A: Yeah.

B: And he's great . . . really nice Eskimo.

A: Is he an Eskimo?

B: Yeah.

A: Look OK—

B: —no.

A: Who's complaining about neighbours?

B: No people really don't like these foreigners coming over and I just think it's unfair . . . and the these Eskimos are really nice . . . I mean the other day he asked me if he could borrow a broom and I said yes over there in the corner and he said what's the corner.

A: Re . . . ha ha . . . really . . . well I find that straightforward . . . people do complain about foreigners coming over to this country.

B: Well, this is it—

A: I mean it's stupid . . . if it wasn't for the foreigners I'll tell you now the majority of the shops around the country wouldn't be open.

B: Well this is true.

A: 'Cos it's so . . . unfortunately it's because of the foreigners like the Indians and everybody . . . will you keep quiet in that new studio please . . . excuse me a second [*song*].

Extract 2 (Phone-in programme: Invicta Radio, Canterbury, Kent; A: Counsellor; B: Caller.)

A: Hello, David.

B: Hi.

A: I wonder if you can tell me something about what your daughter is like at school.

B: Very good . . . er . . . the reports we get back . . . no problems and . . . er . . . really intelligent—

A: And friendships ... and friendships?

B: Er ... not too many friendships I'm afraid ... we've only li-moved up to this area in the last two years.

A: Erm ... was sh ... when at the previous area how were friendships then?

B: Very good.

A: Erm.

B: Er ... but she was still a bit of a problem ... not as much as she is now.

A: Erm ... it it is of course extremely difficult to know what's going on in your every individual case ... you say ... you've actually had got a bit of advice?

B: Oh yes.

A: Erm.

B: We've gone for about five or six sessions with the er ... child psychiatry department.

A: Yes.

B: And ... obviously the end response it er ... upsets my wife so much that we're ending up quarrelling and then we're ... you know ... there's a family problem.

A: Erm ... how ... how does it make your wife feel then?

B: Well obviously ... I mean ... if she's got a child that's er ... doesn't—

A: —Oh, yeah right.

B: Doesn't do what she's told ... or she's disobedient.

A: Yeah yeah?

B: Insolent.

A: Yeah?

B: You know ... but I leave that one to you.

A: Well yes yeah ... I clearly don't know whether I'm able to help you ...

TASKS

1) Record a television or radio programme which is predominantly, or even completely, unscripted. (For example, a radio 'phone-in' programme, or TV interview, particularly an 'on-the-spot' eye witness or comment type, or a 'chat show' which is semi-scripted.) Transcribe a part of it that seems to be interesting in the way the participants are using language, and try to account for what's going on *socially, psychologically* and *linguistically*. Which force do you find the strongest in your extracts?

2) Collect a series of newspaper texts on a topic or particular story. Note the ways in which the stories include and exclude details, and the way in which they are constructed, so as to present you with a particular opinion or point of view. How 'conversational' are the texts? For example, what is the balance between reported and quoted elements? Do they encourage your (or another reader's) participation?

4

SOME ALTERNATIVE WAYS OF INVESTIGATING LANGUAGE

The purpose of these activities is to investigate the 'unconscious' side of our knowledge about language and the ways in which language works. These activities can be used to generate ideas about a topic before examining it more analytically; the analytical activities can then be employed to add to or verify the ideas already generated.

The activities can also be used in the event of a 'block' about a particular aspect of language. Often, thinking 'laterally' about a point enables us to see the point afresh and develop new insights about it. The activities can also be used to 'loosen up' before tackling more abstract ideas.

ACTIVITY 4.1

'Animals'

Often when we are trying to explain our thoughts about an object or an event or process, we use the expression 'It's a funny sort of animal' (or similar). Think about various items of English grammar or description. What sort of animal do you think *the article* is?

Note the reasons for your choice. Can you specify a particular animal? What are its characteristics? Why are they like the article? Compare your ideas with those of a partner. Other items to focus on as animals could include

- modal auxiliaries
- question words
- adjectives
- adverbs
- prepositions.

(As a variation, you might want to think about types of car, weather, film stars, types of fruit (or food), etc.)

ACTIVITY 4.2

Create a machine
If we likened language to a machine, what part do you think each of the following would play in the machine? Would the machine be able to produce something? If so, what would it produce? Explain your reasoning:

- verbs
- nouns
- adjectives
- adverbs
- prepositions
- articles
- other elements of language.

Draw a labelled picture/diagram of your 'language machine'.

ACTIVITY 4.3

Shapes
What sorts of *shape* do you think various parts of language have? Are the shapes *regular* or *irregular*? Do they have a specific number of sides or faces? Or are they multifaceted? Are the shapes jagged or relatively uniform? Why do you think so? Think, for example, about *prepositions*.

ACTIVITY 4.4

Textures
Do various aspects of English have *texture*, or are textures brought to mind by the various elements? For example, what sort of texture do you associate with *conditional* clauses? Does the texture tell us how the conditional relates to other aspects of the language? Or does the texture tell us about how easy or difficult it is to account for the element in question? Why?
   Try this with other clause types, articles, modal auxiliaries, etc.

ACTIVITY 4.5

Advertising

Imagine you and your colleagues are an advertising agency. You have been commissioned to produce advertisements for different aspects of language, in order to encourage more accurate use of these different aspects. The first commission is for an advertisement for compound nouns:

- List the grammatical properties of compound nouns.
- List the lexical features of compound nouns.
- Think of an image which captures the essence of compound nouns.
- Produce your advertising copy and image (you can cut this from a magazine or newspaper) and produce it on an A4 sheet for display.

Be prepared to talk about your ideas.

Note   You can try this activity with other aspects of English, for example, polysemic words or homonyms.

ACTIVITY 4.6

Clause collage

Go through a newspaper and find as many different clause types as you can. Copy them down. Find images and pictures which capture the conceptual idea of each different clause type. For example, what pictures might capture the idea of *cause and effect?* (Often, captions to pictures can provide examples of clause types.)

On a piece of A3 or poster paper, write out your clauses and paste up your images/pictures in an attractive display. Now proceed to the activities in Chapter 2 of this book which investigate clauses.

ACTIVITY 4.7

Computer language

1)   Imagine you are a computer programmer. You have been asked to produce a language which can account for the properties (grammatical and semantic) of different types of words. What properties (in computer code) would you enter into a program which would search a text for nouns, verbs, adverbs, etc.

2)   You have been asked to produce a grammar checker for a wordprocessing program, so that a user could ask the grammar check to examine a piece of text before it was printed out. What elements would you want to include in your grammar check? (For example, would you include information on word order?)

FURTHER READING

The following reference grammars of English will be useful during your investigations of English:

Alexander, L. (1988) *Longman English Grammar* (Harlow:Longman).
Leech, G. (1989) *An A–Z of English Grammar and Usage* (London:Edward Arnold).
Leech, G. and Svartvik, J. (1975) *A Communicative Grammar of English* (London: Longman).
Quirk, R. and Greenbaum, S. (1973) *University Grammar of English* (London: Longman).
Quirk, R., Greenbaum, S., Leech, G. and Svartvik, J. (1972) *A Grammar of Contemporary English* (London:Longman).
Quirk, R., Greenbaum, S., Leech, G. and Svartvik, J. (1985) *A Comprehensive Grammar of the English Language* (Harlow:Longman).
Swan, M. (1980) *Practical English Usage* (Oxford:Oxford University Press).

The following dictionaries will complement the information in the grammars:

Collins Cobuild Essential English Dictionary (1988) (London:Harper Collins).
Longman Dictionary of Contemporary English (1987) (2nd edn) (Harlow: Longman).
Oxford Advanced Learner's Dictionary (1989) (3rd edn) (Oxford:Oxford University Press).

The reader may find the following titles valuable in support of their studies of various parts of this book:

Cook, G. (1989) *Discourse* (Oxford:Oxford University Press). A concise and very readable introduction to the study of discourse. Part I is particularly helpful for users of this book.
Gairns, R and Redman, S. (1986) *Working with Words* (Cambridge:Cambridge University Press). This book is a very good introduction to the problem of teaching vocabulary to second language learners. Contains excellent awareness-raising activities and commentaries.
Yule, G. (1987) *The Study of Language: An Introduction* (Cambridge:Cambridge University Press). This volume introduces all the main areas of language study in a clear and accessible way. It covers, among other topics, grammar, lexis, discourse and pronunciation.

Other books of awareness-raising activities that could be used to supplement the activities in this volume are as follows:

Bolitho, R. and Tomlinson, B. (1980) *Discover English* (London: Heinemann Educational).
Bowers, R., Bamber, B., Straker-Cook, R and Thomas, A. (1987) *Talking About Grammar* (Harlow:Longman).
Tinkel, T. (1989) *Explorations in Language* (Cambridge:Cambridge University Press).

Teachers may find the following very helpful in developing their approach to awareness-raising about language:

Edge, J. (1988) 'Applying linguistics in English language teacher-training for speakers of other languages', *ELT Journal* 42:1. This article discusses the training of English language teachers and discusses the notions of users, analysts and teachers of language.
Hawkins, E. (1984) *Awareness of Language* (Cambridge:Cambridge University Press). This book discusses the notion of language awareness for native speakers of English. It contains useful exercise types, as well as rationale.
James, C and Garrett, P. (eds.) (1991) *Language Awareness in the Classroom* (Harlow: Longman). This collection of papers covers all aspects of language awareness, from definitions to case studies of work at all educational levels in a variety of contexts.

REFERENCES

Alexander, L. (1988) *Longman English Grammar* (Harlow:Longman).

Allen, J.P.B. and van Buren, P. (eds.) (1971) *Chomsky: Selected Readings* (Oxford:Oxford University Press).

Beaumont, D. and Granger, C. (1989) *Heinemann English Grammar* (London: Heinemann).

Bland, S.K. (1988) 'The present progressive in discourse: grammar versus usage revisited'. *TESOL Quarterly* 22/1, pp. 53–68.

Bolitho, R and Tomlinson, B. (1980) *Discover English* (London:Heinemann).

Brown, G. and Yule, G. (1983) *Discourse Analysis* (Cambridge:Cambridge University Press).

Berger, P. and Kellner H. (1981) *Sociology Reinterpreted* (Harmondsworth: Penguin).

Cansdale, G. (1961) *West African Snakes* (London:Longman).

Chalker, S. (1984) 'Why can't someone write a nice, simple grammar?' *ELT Journal*, 38/2, pp. 79–85.

Collins Cobuild English Grammar (1990) (London:Collins).

Cook, G. (1989) *Discourse* (Oxford:Oxford University Press).

Crystal, D. (1971) *Linguistics* (Harmondsworth:Penguin).

Dulay, H., Burt, M. and Krashen, S.D. (1982) *Language Two* (Oxford:Oxford University Press).

Edge, J (1988) 'Applying linguistics in English Language teacher training for speakers of other languages' *ELT Journal* 42/1, pp. 9–13.

Fairclough, N. (1989) *Language and Power* (Harlow:Longman).

Gairns, R. and Redman, S. (1986) *Working with Words* (Cambridge:Cambridge University Press).

Goody, J. (1977) *The Domestication of the Savage Mind* (Cambridge:Cambridge University Press).

Gumperz, J.J. (ed.) (1982) *Language and Social Identity* (Cambridge:Cambridge University Press).

Halliday, M.A.K. (1973) *Explorations in the Functions of Language* (London: Edward Arnold).

Halliday, M.A.K. (1978) *Language as Social Semiotic* (London:Edward Arnold).

Hawkins, E. (1984) *Awareness of Language* (Cambridge:Cambridge University Press).

Holmes, J. (1992) *An Introduction to Sociolinguists* (London:Longman).

Hughes, A. and Trudgill, P. (1987) *English Accents and Dialects* (2nd edn) (London: Edward Arnold).

James,C. A. and Garrett, P. (eds.) (1991) *Language Awareness in the Classroom* (Harlow:Longman).

Jones, D. (1959) *The Pronunciation of English* (3rd edn) (London: University Press).

Kachru, B. (1985) 'Standards, codification and sociolinguistic realism: the English language in the outer circle' in Quirk and Widdowson (eds.)

Kress, G. (1976) (ed.) *Halliday: System and Function in Language* (Oxford:Oxford University Press).

Labov, W. (1970) 'The study of language in its social context' in Pride and Holmes (eds.).

Leech, G.N. (1971) *Meaning and the English Verb* (Harlow:Longman).

Leech, G.N. (1983) *The Principles of Pragmatics* (Harlow:Longman).

Leech, G.N. (1989) *An A–Z of English Grammar and Usage* (London: Edward Arnold).

Leech, G.N. and Svartvik, J. (1975) *A Communicative Grammar of English* (London: Longman).

Lewis, M. (1986) *The English Verb* (Hove:Language Teaching Publications).

Luce, G. G. (1973) *Body Time* (London:Paladin).

Lyons, J. (1968) *Introduction to Theoretical Linguistics* (Cambridge: Cambridge University Press).

Maule, D. (1991) *The Naked Verb* (London:Macmillan).

McCrum, R., Cran, W. and McNeil, R. (1986) *The Story of English* (London:BBC/ Faber and Faber).

Naipaul, S. (1985) *Beyond the Dragon's Mouth* (Tunbridge Wells:Abacus).

Naipaul, V.S. (1963) *The Middle Passage* (Harmondsworth:Penguin).

Neisser, U. (1976) *Cognition and Reality* (London:Freeman).

Palmer, F. (1990) *Grammar* (2nd edn) (Harmondsworth:Penguin).

Parry, H. (1979) *A Use of English Course for West African Students* (London: Macmillan).

Phillipson, R. (1991) *Linguistic Imperialism* (Oxford:Oxford University Press).

Platt, J., Weber, H. and Ho, M.L. (1984) *The New Englishes* (London: Routledge, Kegan Paul).

Prabhu, N.S. (1987) *Second Language Pedagogy* (Oxford:Oxford University Press).

Pride, J.B. and Holmes, J. (eds.) (1972) *Sociolinguistics* (Harmondsworth: Penguin).

Quirk, R. (1985) 'The English language in a global context' in Quirk and Widdowson (eds.)

Quirk, R. and Greenbaum, S. (1973) *University Grammar of English* (London: Longman).

Quirk, R. and Widdowson, H.G. (eds.) (1985) *English in the World* (Cambridge: Cambridge University Press).

Rinvolucri, M. (1984) *Grammar Games* (Cambridge:Cambridge University Press).

Rutherford, W. (1987) *Second Language Grammar:Learning and Teaching* (Harlow: Longman).

Shovel, M. (1985) *Making Sense of Phrasal Verbs* (London:Cassell).

Spolsky, B. (1989) *Conditions for Second Language Learning* (Oxford:Oxford University Press).

Stubbs, M. (1983) *Discourse Analysis* (Oxford:Blackwell).

Tannen, D. (1991) *You just don't understand: Men and women in conversation* (London: Virago).

Todd, L. (1984) *Pidgins and Creoles* (Oxford:Blackwell).

Todd, L. and Hancock, I. (1986) *International English Usage* (London:Croom Helm).

Trudgill, P. (1974) *Sociolinguistics* (Harmondsworth:Penguin).

Trudgill, P. and Hannah, J. (1993) *International English: a Guide to Varieties of Standard English* (3rd edn.) (London:Edward Arnold).

Ur, P. (1989) *Grammar Practice Activities* (Cambridge:Cambridge University Press).

Wallace, C. (1992) *Reading* (Oxford:Oxford University Press).

Wells, J. C. (1982) *Accents of English* (3 Vols) (Cambridge:Cambridge University Press).

Wenden, A. and Rubin, J. (eds.) (1987) *Learner Strategies in Language Learning* (Hemel Hempstead:Prentice Hall).

Widdowson, H. G. (1978) *Teaching Language as Communication* (Oxford: Oxford University Press).

Yule, G (1987) *The Study of Language: An Introduction* (Cambridge:Cambridge University Press).

INDEX

Note: entries in the index refer to main reference points in the book. The user is also referred to the Index of Activities, many of which are cited in bold in this Index.

LIST OF ACTIVITIES